After You Graduate

After You Graduate

Finding and getting work you will enjoy

Leila Roberts

Open University Press

Open University Press
McGraw-Hill Education
McGraw-Hill House
Shoppenhangers Road
Maidenhead
Berkshire
England
SL6 2QL

email: enquiries@openup.co.uk
world wide web: www.openup.co.uk

and Two Penn Plaza, New York, NY 10121-2289, USA

First published 2006

A catalogue record of this book is available from the British Library

ISBN-10: 0 335 21793 1 (pb) 0 335 21794 X (hb)
ISBN-13: 978 0 335 21793 9 (pb) 978 0 335 21794 6 (hb)

Library of Congress Cataloging-in-Publication Data
CIP data applied for

Typeset by RefineCatch Limited, Bungay, Suffolk
Printed in the UK by Bell and Bain Ltd, Glasgow

Contents

Acknowledgements

My thanks to all the students and graduates who have given me ideas and encouragement when writing this book; to the staff of the Careers Service at York St John College and to Val Butcher for her time and expert advice.

This book owes a huge debt to careers advisers and others who have worked in this field before me: the Further information section should lead readers to many of these authoritative sources of help and advice.

1

Introduction: what's in this book for you?

Students often say they're studying for a degree because a degree 'leads to a better job'. At the same time everyone knows of graduates, some with good degrees, who are unemployed or employed in jobs they don't like.

In other words, there's considerable confusion. Does a degree automatically lead to a better job? Is it, in a memorable phrase, a 'passport to the middle classes'? Or is it just the beginning? Is it an irrelevance? How do you move from being a successful student to having a job you enjoy?

Some students don't use their university careers service or pick up books like this, either because of a sunny assumption that a degree will open any doors or because of an unspoken fear that looking at 'graduate jobs' means accepting some conformist straitjacket. A fear that there is a limited and tight number of 'graduate' jobs – most of which involve wearing suits and climbing (metaphorical) ladders. *'I think career is a big scary word (certainly frightens the life out of me)'* wrote Andy, a recent student. Following Andy's advice I'll state here that my definition of 'career' might not be what you expect!

The good news is that there are many opportunities for graduates (and not just in conventional 'jobs'); tried and tested ways of identifying what type of work you will enjoy; and proven strategies to increase your chances of getting it. This book will take you through these processes from 'career choice' to making effective applications, and beyond.

It takes you from asking, 'What is a graduate job?' (Chapter 2) to helping you identify what sort of work you might enjoy (Chapter 3). It then explores how to find opportunities (Chapter 4) and goes on to help you in how to present yourself to employers (Chapter 5). This book concludes, in Chapter 6, by looking at lifetime career skills.

The more you understand about the world of graduate employment, the better prepared you will be to carve out an individual and personal career for yourself, and make it one that you will enjoy.

This is very much your own journey. It will probably involve a lot of work – more than you expect. It will require perseverance, flexibility and effort. You will have to use many of the skills, intellectual and personal qualities which you have developed throughout your studies. Because work is so important to our overall happiness, this journey is also supremely worth doing.

> *A life, your values, your pride and your living all in one.*
> (Tamsin, a young graduate, describing her work)

- How important is it for you to find work you enjoy?
- How much time and effort are you prepared to put in to get it?

> Here are the reactions of students who piloted the exercises in this book:
>
> *Overall I feel that I have learned a lot . . . About myself and where I can go when June comes and I walk out of this place. The thought was very daunting before but I can honestly say that I am looking forward to it now.*
> (Tom)
>
> *This . . . has allowed me to reflect, take stock, and plan my future.*
> (Lucy)
>
> *One of the best things I could have done . . . I feel a lot happier in myself. It feels like a huge weight has been lifted off me . . .*
> (Katie)

Most of the boxed quotes and case examples in this book are from students I have worked with (names and some small details have been changed for reasons of confidentiality).

Summary

The more you understand about the world of graduate employment, career choice and job-hunting, the better prepared you will be to carve out an individual and personal career for yourself, a career that you will enjoy.

2

What do graduates do?

What is a graduate job? • *What do graduates in your subject do?* •
Summary

What is a graduate job?

What is a graduate job? How do you recognise it? Does it imply high pay,
lots of responsibility, working for a big company – or is it simply any job
that a graduate does? To examine the 'graduate job' we need to analyse
(and challenge) some popular assumptions. This is important because
wrong assumptions about graduate jobs can be so unhelpful they actually prevent you from finding work you might enjoy.

What is a graduate?

A silly question – someone with a degree! But for generations the word
'graduate' implied an educational elite, one of a small number of highly
educated people, usually male. Things aren't, of course, like that any
more, but shades of this original meaning still colour many of our
assumptions, especially those concerning graduate expectations.

In the early 1960s only 6 percent of under-21s in the UK went on to
higher education: today that is nearer 43 percent and the intention is to
increase it further. That is an enormous difference. Also, undergraduates
are studying a more varied range of courses than ever before. No longer
do degree courses simply reflect the subjects studied at school (physics,

chemistry, history . . .) there are now degree programmes in an amazing variety of subjects (journalism, equine studies, sports science. . .)

Because of this, graduate employment has changed. Graduates now do a much wider range of jobs for a much more varied range of employers than they did in the past. Some jobs which used to be non-graduate now routinely ask for graduates (but the jobs will probably have changed). At the same time, many graduates go into work where a degree is not a specific requirement.

Which organizations employ graduates?

There are now more graduates, from a wider range of subjects, which means that the type of employers recruiting these graduates is changing. Information on 'graduate employers' in the press and on radio and TV usually focuses on big companies: financial institutions, major manufacturers and retailers, for example. The free graduate careers directories you can pick up from careers services usually feature big employers with regular graduate recruitment programmes.

In fact only about 20 percent of graduates are in the sort of 'high flier' jobs featured in the media. Many graduates work for small or medium sized organizations, or are self-employed. (It is predicted that smaller organizations will become vital to economic growth and will be important recruiters of graduates.)

When I use the term 'organisation' it's easy to think of 50 people in a glass-fronted building with lots of desks. However, I'm using the term to mean a group of people employed in a related task – and this could be a small software business, a catering company or an artist's studio. . . Although there are still designated graduate training schemes in large organizations, very many graduates will find employment with smaller, more diverse organizations – or they will be self-employed.

How much do graduates get paid?

The idea that a 'graduate employer' can only be a big household-name company is plainly wrong. Of course these companies, and other large organizations (like the Armed Forces, NHS and Civil Service) do employ many graduates, but they are not by any means the only ones. However, 'graduate employer' still often conjures up ideas of big organizations and, often, very big salaries. Alas, this isn't always true either.

Many students have unrealistic ideas of graduate starting salaries (one group I worked with identified a 'graduate job' as involving a chauffeur-driven car!) A graduate recruiter reading this manuscript commented that many employers are put off by applicants whose salary expectations wildly exceed what can be offered. These unrealistic expectations are often based on press reports. Salary surveys in the media often give 'graduate starting salaries' but don't say that they are getting their information from only a limited number of big employers. I looked at two recent surveys: one gave graduate salaries as starting at £18,000 per annum with a median of £20,800 (but what it didn't say was that the survey was based on information from large prestigious companies). The other survey showed a range of graduate starting salaries, from £5000 to £40,000 per annum, with most clustering between £10,000 and £20,000. In other words, just as graduates work for all types and sizes of organizations, so they earn widely varying salaries. A look in the vacancies pages of national newspapers will give you an idea of how very different salaries can be.

Over a lifetime graduates can expect to earn more than non-graduates (especially graduate women compared with non-graduate women – although they still lag behind graduate men). However, these figures are looking at the careers of people who entered the workforce when graduates were a small minority. We simply don't know how, when graduates approach 50 percent of a cohort, they will fare in terms of prospects and prosperity in the future.

But why are some poorly paid graduate jobs still very competitive? Why do people go to university and study only to earn less than they might have done if they had gone into a factory straight from school? Do people work only for money or is there something else in the equation? Many graduates say the benefit of their degree is that it gave them the opportunity to find a fulfilling job. But what do we mean by fulfilling? What need is being fulfilled?

What is a fulfilling job?

> *Man has his labour of body or mind which declares his dignity.*
> (John Milton)

Our culture has an ambivalent attitude to work: on the one hand people moan about it as a chore or a grind, but on the other hand we feel sorry for people who are unemployed. We understand, if we don't always acknowledge it, that if you have work you enjoy it can be a source of happiness and fulfilment.

A group of women who were among the first winners of the National Lottery were asked if they were going to give up their jobs? No, they said, they enjoyed their jobs – *because they really liked working with each other.*

People get all sorts of rewards from work, not only material ones. Here are some things work can provide:

- A routine
- Money
- Status
- A chance to be creative
- Stability
- A feeling of belonging
- The ability to influence or change things
- The chance to contribute to something
- The opportunity to learn
- Respect from others
- A new and wider range of friends
- Stimulation
- Challenge: emotional, physical, intellectual . . .
- A label, or social identity
- (One of my students added, 'A chance to get away from the kids. . .'!)

Our culture very rarely discusses this, but work seems to be fundamental to our well-being, and even unpaid work can bring rewards. Often the idea of a 'graduate job' has a suggestion of 'a job that brings me personal rewards' – not just drudgery. It is important then, that you identify *what you personally want from a job in terms of your own individual values.* These may well be different from those of your best friends or your family. (Chapter 3, 'What does success mean to you?' (pp. 20–29) will help you identify what you personally want from your work.)

So, a graduate job often implies a personally rewarding job, but this means different things for different people. Graduates are sometimes groping towards this idea when they say, 'graduates have a career rather than a job'. But what do we mean by a 'career'?

What is a career?

The dictionary defines 'career' as:

- a path or progress through life; or
- a profession or occupation chosen as one's life's work.

For many graduates, the second definition is what springs to mind. 'Career' seems to imply several things, including:

- progression upwards – often through promotion; and
- choosing a field of work and staying in it.

However, this can be unhelpful, for several reasons:

1 Not everyone has, or wants, a job that brings the opportunity for promotion.
   Many larger organizations have different grades, and employees can progress upward – but not all organizations give you this opportunity. Also, there has been a recent trend in some organizations for 'flatter', less hierarchical and more task-orientated organizational structures where the 'career ladder' in its traditional sense has almost disappeared.
   Not every employee wants promotion. Some people are very happy to stay within their 'comfort zone' – they would much rather do the same job in the same way for years than face the stress of new challenges.
2 Some people don't want to stay in the same job or with the same employer. Sometimes this is because they want the opportunity to learn something new; sometimes they would just like a change. 'Career' for them isn't about progression, it's about variety.
3 Some put different 'jobs' together, like pieces in a jig-saw. Just as some students study and do part-time paid work to pay the bills, some people put different jobs together – one job might provide rewards that the other doesn't.

> Kieran was a freelance computer-aided designer whose second job was as a physical therapist with a football club. The jobs were very different, and the therapy provided rewards not offered by the better-paid computer job.

Different people have different career paths. Women, for instance, have often taken career breaks to bring up children; this option is increasingly open to men too.

Career patterns can be unpredictable: partly because of personal preferences or changing personal circumstances; and partly because the world we live in is one of rapid change and uncertainty.

How graduate jobs are changing

The world we live in is changing faster than ever before. New technologies, faster communications, and social and environmental pressures all mean that the work we do is subject to constant change. (Ask around – you will probably find people you know who have at some time been made redundant, or whose jobs have changed enormously over the years.)

New technologies mean that new industries are springing up all the time – look at the rise of the mobile phone industry, or genetics. New technologies create new jobs, or they change the way old jobs are done. For example, computer generated images means that film makers can stage huge battle scenes without employing thousands of 'extras'; email and the Internet mean that people can work from home and still keep in touch with the office. Who can predict what technologies will be developed in the next decades? As technologies change, jobs change, and the people doing them have to adapt.

The rise of globalization has enormous implications for jobs. These days manufacturers can move production to countries where the labour force is cheaper. Call centres, once a growth industry in the UK, are being moved to countries such as India: phone a mail order catalogue or gas company and your enquiry could be being handled in Mumbai.

Political, social and environmental trends also affect employment. The late twentieth century saw a huge increase in women in the workforce: partly as a result of women's emancipation, partly because rising house prices meant more families needed to be dual-income. The threat of terrorism has led to the expansion of security services at all levels. The rise in litigation for personal injury has boosted the sector concerned with health and safety. Global warming will demand new technologies, new social strategies and therefore new jobs.

Changes in business practices can also impact on jobs: recent trends include 'downsizing' (cutting staff numbers) and 'de-layering' (cutting hierarchies). Downsizing has meant that many people who once worked for large organizations have found themselves 'hived off' into working for small satellite companies which the big company 'bought in' to fulfil certain tasks. In the 1990s some big graduate recruiters scrapped their formal graduate training schemes and instead recruited from agencies. Who can predict the next round of changes?

Over the years many pundits have made predictions about the future of work: these have ranged from the idea that by the twenty-first century we all would have more leisure than we would know what to do with (if only!) to that of the end of 'the job' (in other words we'll all be on short-term contracts to fulfil specific tasks). What we do know for sure is that we simply don't know what the future will bring.

The winds of change will affect us all, we just don't know how or when. This is why governments around the world are keen on educating more graduates: graduates, by definition, are people who can learn. In a fast changing world, few of us can expect to be doing the same job in the same way ten years from now. In fact recent research in the US predicted that graduates could face up to 11 job changes in their working lives. This is why my own definition of 'career' is the first that I listed from the dictionary – that of a path or progress through life. And paths can be as various as the people walking them.

If this is challenging, it's also exciting. Graduates today have far greater choices than ever before in terms of jobs, employers, career structure – even the countries they live in. Many recent graduates are questioning the high commitment, long hours culture of today's workplace and are actively seeking alternative career paths. 'Career management' isn't necessarily about climbing the corporate ladder: it's about achieving your own preferred career path.

Many students worry about choosing what type of work they want to do when they graduate – it seems to be a once in a lifetime, binding decision. But this is, for most people, not true. The world of employment is now so fluid that most of us can expect to have to change employer and to do different jobs in our working lives. Rather than having a crystal ball telling you 'what to be' when you graduate, it would be much more useful to learn career skills which will see you through an increasingly unpredictable working life. The more you know about career choice and job finding, the more likely you are to find your own preferred way.

Summary

- Graduates are going into a much wider range of occupations than ever before.
- Graduates work for all sizes of employer – including working for themselves.
- Graduate salaries vary as much as graduate jobs.
- A graduate job often implies a personally rewarding job, but this will be different for different people.

- In a fast changing world, jobs will change; graduates are needed because they are adaptable and can learn new things.
- The more 'career skills' you have, the more likely you are to find your own preferred way.

What do graduates in your subject do?

A graduate job, some students think, is one which is *necessarily connected with the subject of their degree.* Wrong.

You will have studied your degree subject for several years. You have been part of a cohort which identified itself as 'biologists' or 'linguists' or whatever; in other words you will have developed a sense of *identity* and *expertise* linked to your subject. This sometimes makes it harder to look 'out of the loop' at occupations which don't necessarily have any obvious connection with your degree subject. However, it can be limiting not to. There may be jobs out there that you will love, but you're not researching them because they don't specifically relate to your degree subject. Sometimes it pays to be flexible: you may find your degree is useful to you in ways you have never thought of.

Of course graduates do go into jobs which are related to their degrees, but not always and not inevitably. Some otherwise excellent careers courses offered in universities try to present themselves as vocational by inappropriately trying to relate possible job opportunities to the degree subject. This is fine if you're studying Occupational Therapy, but can be unhelpful if you're doing French. Trying to make a direct connection between particular subjects and possible occupations can make graduates feel a failure if their ultimate jobs bear no relation to their degree subject (in reality, this is very common).

On a visit to a gas company I met some young managers. A few seemed oddly embarrassed about their jobs, which puzzled me: they had done very well to get these posts in the face of stiff competition and they seemed to enjoy the jobs, so what was the problem? It turned out that they felt they had somehow failed because the job had 'nothing to do' with their degree subjects. It bothered me that these bright successful young people should – for no good reason – feel like failures.

Of course there are many students who find employment in an area directly related to their degree courses. Engineers become engineers, medical students become physicians, some linguists become interpreters and translators. . . But it is also true that every year between 40 percent and 70 percent of all graduate vacancies ask for a degree in *any discipline*, because the knowledge content of the student's degree is immaterial to the position.

What's so great about being a graduate?

There are many reasons for wanting to study at university: some students specifically aim 'to get a better job', others value personal growth and the chance to widen their horizons. Some love the chance to be learning, others just fancy being a student – putting off the evil day of having to work full-time!

But why should employers ask for graduates? Why are governments around the world trying to get more and more people into higher education? What's so great about being a graduate?

Graduates are assumed to have 'transferable' personal and intellectual skills: skills which can be used in different situations and contexts. These may include being able to:

- Work independently, manage their own time and take responsibility for their own learning.
- Research information.
- Analyse complex information – for example, to clarify underlying assumptions or values.
- Synthesize different ideas and information.
- Evaluate information and make judgements about it.
- Think about the wider consequences or implications of specific actions or policies.
- Communicate effectively, orally and in writing.
- Work with others on group tasks.
- Learn to live with people from different cultures and backgrounds.
- Be independent: in living and learning.
- Develop problem-solving skills.
- Manage their money.
- Be adaptable and willing to learn new things.

EXERCISE 2.1

Looking at the above list of graduate skills, could you give examples of how you have developed these skills? (E.g., you might have developed your communication and team working skills through doing a group presentation).

Higher education isn't just about assimilating information about your subject; it's being able to use your intellectual and personal skills in flexible ways which could be useful in very many different contexts.

EXERCISE 2.2

What have you learned when at university that is *not directly connected* with your degree studies? (E.g., budgeting, organizing your time, managing rotas, travelling independently, etc.) Make a list of some of the things you have learned.

(TIP: Keep the notes from these exercises as they will be useful when writing your CV and application forms.)

But what do graduates in your subject do?

Many students undertake a degree course with a specific job in mind but never research what people graduating in their subject *actually* go into. Recent research suggests that many graduates regret having studied their degree subject – possibly because they assumed that a particular degree was an automatic passport into a particular occupation. But:

- English graduates don't just have to teach, or write.
- History majors don't all work in museums.
- Chemistry graduates don't have to become research or analytical chemists.

Here are a few things that recently graduated *chemists* did: scientific research; marketing and sales; teaching; clerical work; nursing; retail; general management . . .

Historians went into many types of jobs including: the armed forces; public sector management; marketing and sales; teaching; business and finance . . .

> Some time ago a young man came to my house conducting a transport survey. We got chatting and he said he was an unemployed graduate doing temporary work. I asked him about himself and he said he'd graduated in History. I was sympathetic – it was a time of high unemployment – and I asked how long had he been unemployed? 'Seven years,' he replied. He asked about my husband and me – what did we do? What did we graduate in? 'English Literature,' I said, and I worked in a careers service. My husband's degree was French and he was a tax inspector. The young man's comments as he left told me why he had been unemployed for seven years. 'Goodbye,' he said, '*and I hope you get graduate jobs soon.*'
>
> I think he was looking for a job ad which specified: 'Must have detailed knowledge of the 100 Years War!'

The largest numbers of *media studies* graduates in 2004 were in secretarial and clerical occupations, followed by retail and catering, then PR and media. (This may reflect the fact that the 'snapshot' of graduate destinations is taken fairly soon after graduation and many students may simply be 'ticking over', paying off their debts and looking for longer-term work.)

Most *electrical engineers*, unsurprisingly, became professional engineers, but many were scattered in a range of occupations including information technology; the armed forces; marketing and sales; commercial and public sector management . . .

Psychology graduates' jobs included: commercial and industrial management; health and childcare; clerical and secretarial work; retail; teaching; marketing and sales . . .

(Some research suggests that many graduates are in their early thirties before they move into a type of work they think they will stay in. In fact some evidence suggests that many graduates take any job after graduation in order to pay off their debts.)

How can you find out what people graduating in your subject actually do? Log on to the website, 'What Do Graduates Do?', at www.prospects.ac.uk

One of the few students I've taught who had a strong vocation was a Theatre and Film Studies student. She had always wanted to be a midwife. She reasoned that she shouldn't go into nursing straight from school – she needed some life experience, so she chose to do a degree in a subject she really enjoyed. After she graduated she went into nurse training.

The 'graduate profile'

During your studies you may have been encouraged to compile a portfolio of your studies and achievements – it may be called something like the 'graduate portfolio' or 'profile'. If you have done this it will be an invaluable source of material for your job-hunting. It should also have encouraged you to reflect upon what you are learning, beyond just the knowledge content of your degree.

REFLECTION 2.1

How have you developed during your higher education studies?

* What new skills do you have?
* Are you different now as a person from when you started? If so, in what ways?

Your career as a graduate

The biggest difference between student life and work is that as a student you have responsibility (probably) only for yourself and your own learning. In work what you do (or don't do) may greatly affect other people. Most graduates have a steep 'learning curve' when going into their first job. However, this is one of the reasons people employ graduates: graduates are people who know how to learn.

We have seen in the first part of this chapter that graduates go into a wider range of jobs with a wider range of employers than ever before. They will probably also be required to change jobs more often than were previous generations, because of the rapid changes in working life. It is therefore imperative that, as a graduate, you develop the career management skills to enable you to cope with these choices and changes. These include:

- Being able to evaluate jobs and understand why you may prefer some over others (see Chapter 3).
- Be able to use your graduate research skills to identify opportunities. (Chapter 4).
- Be able to present yourself positively on paper, on the phone and in person (see Chapter 5).
- Be able to manage changes and transitions (Chapter 6).

Summary

- A high proportion of graduate vacancies ask for a degree in any subject.
- Many employers are more interested in the intellectual or other achievements of candidates, their personalities and personal qualities, than in their degree subject or classification.
- You are not a failure if your job isn't obviously related to your degree: it's a common situation for graduates.
- You will probably have to develop many new skills to meet the challenges of working life.
- A degree can significantly add to your quality of life, and not just in material ways.

3

What kind of work might you enjoy?

*Choosing a 'career' • What does success mean to you? • Your skills •
Your personality • Your interests • Your personal preferences •
Putting it all together • Using this information to choose job areas to
investigate • Getting help • Summary*

Choosing a 'career'

Students often say they sign up for careers courses because, 'I have no idea what I want to do'. When friends and family ask about your future it's easy to feel anxious and demoralized if you don't have a ready reply: it's assumed that you *ought* to be able to say, 'I want to be a . . . nurse/ social worker/analytical chemist', etc. You can feel inadequate if you can't come up with an easy answer. Be reassured that *very many graduates are in the same position,* and it's not necessarily a bad position to be in, because it means you will be encouraged to think about your future and to develop a range of career management skills which will benefit you in the long term.

> *The immediate future seems very shaky: I feel as though everyone else knows exactly what they are going to do and are all very confident they are going to achieve their goals. I'm not sure what my goals are . . .*
>
> (Annabel)

Of course, it's great if you *do* have a clear idea of what you want to do. If you are looking for a professional post as a chemical engineer, say, or know you want residential social work, then you probably know what job advertisements to look for, and which employers you might contact. You might want to skip to Chapters 4 (Researching opportunities) or 5 (Presenting yourself effectively). However, it may be worth doing some of the exercises in this chapter (especially Exercises 3.4–3.9) because these may help you make high quality applications.

'What do you want to do?' – the unhelpful question

Let's think about the, 'What do you want to do?' question, because it does cause such anxiety. This question is difficult for all sorts of reasons, not least because it assumes several things which may not necessarily be true. Let's look at these faulty assumptions:

1 *You're going to choose one job or 'career' path which you will stay in for most of your working life.*

   As we've already seen, that's unlikely. Most of us can expect to make several job changes. Your entry-level job may not be the job of your dreams – but might lead to it.

2 *There are a limited number of (clearly labelled) jobs.*

   In fact there are thousands and thousands of different jobs – many that you or I have never heard of. New ones are being created all the time. (A recent student of mine got a job researching suitable properties for period films and TV. What job title would this have?)

3 *Job titles are clear and accurate.*

   Job titles can be misleading: a classics student got a job as a systems engineer with a computer company – it didn't involve engineering as normally understood. A window cleaner on a radio programme was laughing that he was now called a 'visibility technician'! Do you know what a 'gaffer' or 'best boy' does?

4 *We're all going to have strictly defined jobs with clear job descriptions.*

   Some pundits say that increasingly work will be organized flexibly, with people moving from task to task as required (some organizations already do this). Or that many of us will be employed on short-term contracts to complete specific projects, rather than being given a long-term job.

5 *People always choose a career positively, as they would a vocation.*

Whoever said, 'I want to be a customer services manager'? – but many people are happily doing this job.

So, finding work you enjoy is more complicated than choosing between a pack of job titles. There is a world of opportunities out there, probably more so than ever before – which can be both exhilarating and daunting. This section aims to give you the first part of your 'route map', a portfolio of information about you yourself; what you want and what you can offer.

How do people choose work they will enjoy?

There are many theories on what influences our career choice, from the bizarre (it depends on how your mum cuddled you) to the obvious (lots of people go into jobs that their parents do). Perhaps the most useful route to successful job choice goes something like this:

1 *Me*: Analyse your skills, personal values, personality traits, interests, etc. (covered in this chapter).
2 *The job*: Investigate the requirements of different jobs in terms of skills required, useful personality traits, etc. (we will look at this in chapter 4).
3 *Making a match*: Match the two. Where there is a good match it's assumed you stand a good chance of liking the job.

This approach seems to make sense. Students who say they have absolutely no idea what they want to do often have very clear ideas about what they *don't* want to do. This is an excellent start.

Look at these jobs:

firefighter	psychiatric nurse	probation officer
garden designer	statistician	tax officer
systems analyst	accountant	journalist
lecturer	librarian	singer
transport manager		

There are probably some (if not all) that you know you definitely would *not* want to do, either because you couldn't (you don't have the skills) or there are aspects of the job that would not appeal at all. The task now is to analyse *exactly* what you might enjoy in a job and what you definitely wouldn't; then the picture will become much clearer.

The rest of this section will look at ways of analysing yourself and what you hope to find in a job you will enjoy. Unlike Chapter 2, this will involve you in a lot of work – it's not a matter of me conveying information, in this section the information will be provided by you. Some of the exercises will be quite time consuming but *the more effort you put into them the more benefit you will gain.*

REFLECTION 3.1

- How important is it to find work you will enjoy?
- How much effort are you prepared to put into it?

I feel I have gained a lot more than I expected . . . you get out what you have put in. I worked hard [on these exercises] but I enjoyed it and feel it's helped me a lot.

(Jo, final year undergraduate)

What does success mean to you?

If you follow your bliss, you put yourself on a kind of track which has been there all the while waiting for you, and the life that you ought to be living is the one you are living.

(Joseph Campbell)

This part of the chapter is intended to help you identify your personal source of fulfilment – what *you* want to get out of your work. This is an important consideration in identifying what sort of work you might enjoy.

We saw in Chapter 2 that 'work' can be a source of fulfilment in many different ways. It is important to realize that different people want different things from work. The media often talk about pay as if it's the only thing that motivates people, but this isn't true. Although, of course, most people would *like* to be very well paid, not everyone would value that above all other considerations. Many jobs in nature conservation, for example, are not particularly well paid but they attract many applicants – for reasons unconnected with money.

Often graduates have a gut feeling about different kinds of work, or different employers, sensing that they would like to work with one or not another, but finding it difficult to articulate their reasons why.

> *I had been thinking of a career in advertising. It seemed to fit what I wanted from a job – creativity and the rest. But I always had a feeling it wasn't right. When I did [this] exercise I realized why – my key value was 'personally valuable work' and advertising wouldn't fulfil that for me.*
> (Bronwen)

Exercise 3.1 below will help you identify and articulate *your* key work values, that is, what motivates you in a job. This is important because, if you're doing a job where your most important personal value is not met, you will most likely feel dissatisfied or unhappy.

Your key values

 EXERCISE 3.1

Look at the statements below. Give each one a mark out of 5 (5 = strongly agree 3 = neutral 1 = strongly disagree). Note your score beside each statement.

1 It's important to have a steady job with a good pension.
2 I prefer to be in charge.
3 My position in the organization is important to me.
4 I wouldn't enjoy work where I don't like the people.
5 I like to be seen to have specialist knowledge.
6 I would hate a job where I couldn't do things in new and different ways.
7 I work best if given freedom to organize my workload myself.
8 I wouldn't want to work for an organization whose aims I don't believe in.

9   I like to put my original mark on what I'm doing.
10 I want a job with 'perks' such as a car or an expense account.
11 I want the power to decide how things are done.
12 It's important to feel my job is secure.
13 It's important to me that my work is useful.
14 I enjoy feeling highly knowledgeable about my field.
15 I would like a job that people respect.
16 I want to contribute to something important.
17 Work is a place to make friends and socialise.
18 I would hate a job that gives me little personal independence.
19 If I had to choose between two jobs I'd always go for the one that paid the most, irrespective of any other considerations.
20 I need to feel financially secure.
21 I enjoy motivating others.
22 With whom I work is as important as what I do.
23 I need to feel my job is valuable to society.
24 Success means earning a high salary.
25 I like people to see me as 'the person to ask'.
26 I want to be seen to be a leader.
27 If I had to choose between two identical jobs I would always take the one in the more prestigious organization.
28 I would like a high level of independence in what I do.
29 I enjoy being an 'expert'.
30 I like the opportunity to think independently.
31 Work is an extension of my family and friends.
32 It's rewarding to be the one who knows how to do things.
33 I want to be recognized for what I do.
34 I value job stability.
35 Good working relationships give me job satisfaction.
36 I want my work to give something to others.
37 If I were offered a 'dream job' but it might be short-term, I would stay with my steady job.
38 I would hate being subordinate and having little control.
39 I need personal space and autonomy in my work.
40 I enjoy seeing new and different ways of doing things.
41 It's important for me to work in a happy team.
42 I would like a job with a long-term career path.
43 I like to express myself in what I do.
44 It's important to me to know a lot about my field.
45 It's important to me to be a high earner.
46 I would enjoy having control over money or people.

47   I would enjoy having rank, or more letters after my name.
48   I would hate to be tightly supervised.
49   My work is an expression of my place in the world and my contribution to it.
50   If I had the chance of a more interesting job that paid a lot less I would never take it.
51   I pride myself on being creative.
52   I would happily change jobs to get more money.
53   My job title is an important 'badge' indicating who I am.
54   I need to be able to decide my own routines and working style.

Now add up your scores for each cluster of questions.

- Total for group C (nos. 2, 11, 21, 26, 38, 46):
- Total for group E (nos. 5, 14, 25, 44, 29):
- Total for group F (nos. 4, 17, 22, 31, 35, 41):
- Total for group I (nos. 6, 9, 30, 40, 43, 51):
- Total for group ID (nos. 7, 18, 28, 39, 48, 54):
- Total for group M (nos. 10, 19, 24, 45, 50, 52):
- Total for group P (nos. 3, 15, 27, 33, 47, 53):
- Total for group S (nos. 1, 12, 20, 34, 37, 42):
- Total for group V (nos. 8, 13, 16, 23, 36, 49):

Look at your highest scores – these will be your most important value or values. (But please note that you know yourself best – if the result feels wrong, change it to one that seems right for you. Ask for feedback from the people who know you best.) Here's what the groups mean:

Group C: Control

If this is your motivator, you like to be in control of people and resources. You will enjoy being in a position to make decisions and affect policies. You would enjoy managerial roles and would like to be near the centre of power. You may well be uncomfortable in a subordinate position but would flourish when you achieved a measure of influence. A doctor with this as a motivator may well look to move to a position when s/he could affect hospital policies.

A student interviewed her boyfriend about his job. He said it was rubbish, he hated it – until the boss went on holiday and suddenly he was in charge. He set about doing things differently, and loved it!

Group E: Experts

These people enjoying having specialist knowledge or abilities. They like to be the person people ask when they need to know about a specific topic or how to perform an unusual task. The expertise could be in any field – from fashion to plumbing, heart disease to horses: satisfaction comes from depth of knowledge. A doctor with this key value may want to become an acknowledged expert in a particular speciality, disease or treatment. (Note that the expertise may be gained after you graduate – and it need not necessarily be in the same area as your degree subject.)

Group F: Friendship

If this is your motivator you will be looking for enriching relationships as part of your work. You like cooperation and continuity in relationships. 'Friendship' people would be unhappy if they disliked their co-workers, even if all other aspects of the job were good. Their commitment is to their work colleagues more than to the job or organization. A doctor with this as a motivator would perhaps look to work in a harmonious team.

Group I: Imagination and creativity

People with this as a motivator enjoy thinking 'out of the loop', looking for different ways of doing things, and having their originality acknowledged. They often prefer to work in small groups or by themselves, and would hate large bureaucracies with prescribed ways of doing things. Their creativity could express itself in any field. A doctor with this motivator might want to undertake research or look for innovation in his/her practice – this could be in anything from the design of the waiting room to integrating 'alternative' therapies with a conventional practice.

Group ID: Independence

If this is your highest value you will look for situations where you can control your work as much as possible – in terms of what you do, or when or where you do it. You will hate being tightly monitored, and following strict protocols will feel like being in prison; but you may well be very highly self-motivated. You will probably rebel against perceived restrictions. People with this value often prefer to work alone or in small groups where they have a lot of freedom of action – perhaps by having their own business. A doctor with this key value may like to work solo or in a small practice.

Group M: Money and 'perks'

People with this motivator will be attracted by high pay, perks, company cars, etc. They may well 'trade off' aspects of the job they don't like to get high pay or bonuses. Many City 'high fliers' will be motivated by this value: accepting stress, pressure, long hours, etc. in order to accumulate wealth. A doctor with this as a motivator may well choose to work in private practice, or in a high paying country.

(A word of caution: In these days of high student debt, I have found that many more graduates than previously have identified 'money' as a primary value. This may be an entirely valid result; however, it may equally reflect anxieties more than real long-term preferences. Imagine if you had no debt – would you still have given the same answers? If not, if you think 'money' has been artificially inflated, you may consider whether it really is a key motivator for you.)

Group P: Prestige

You will like to be seen as important in your workplace or in the wider community. Your status may be shown through rank or job title, in symbols (on uniforms or by having a bigger office), or by the fact you mix with important people. You will enjoy having a high profile and would hate to be in the background, overlooked. Your position might be within a very small world but so long as you are a 'big fish' you will be satisfied. A doctor with this as a key value might look to be a consultant or value the title 'doctor' in the wider community.

Group S: Security

Someone with this as their highest value will look for reliability over excitement, predictability over change. They want to feel assured that their job is safe and their income regular. They will not want to take unnecessary risks. They would prefer to know what to expect, and would find unpredictability and rapid change stressful. A doctor with this as a value would look for a long-term job, or clear career structure, so s/he would be able to imagine what they might be doing in ten years' time.

Simon was offered a job with a bigger organization than the one he currently was in, with increased pay. However it was a three year contract, whereas his present job was permanent. In addition, he wasn't sure of what he would actually be doing in the new job. On reflection, he preferred to stay where he was.

Group V: Personally valuable work

You want to contribute to something which you feel is important or valuable. This group will be strongly guided by moral or intellectual values. They may make sacrifices in order to fulfil their own deepest beliefs. Their decisions may be incomprehensible to others who do not share their convictions. They would feel crushed if they worked for an organization whose aims they thought were trivial or socially harmful. A doctor with this as a key value would find satisfaction from patient welfare and may well work in unfashionable places, or would perhaps take on an educative role.

> Frances left her secure and well paid job with a software company in order to do two years' Voluntary Service Overseas in Nepal, where she was paid the same wage as locals (very little, in Western terms). She did it because it provided her with rewards that she valued: she felt she was helping; she felt challenged and changed by the experience; and she felt she was 'giving something back'.

> I once did this exercise with a group of Theology and Business Studies students. Unsurprisingly, there were many more Ms among the business students and many more Vs among the theologians. It was quite illuminating how each group was amazed by the other's values!

 REFLECTION 3.2

Values can change over your lifetime but, for many people, they seem to remain fairly consistent.

 EXERCISE 3.2

Try the above exercise on members of your family. Ask individual members if they are happy in their work and ask them to do the questionnaire. Does the job fulfil their key values or not? Is there any connection between that and their level of satisfaction with their job? Try your friends too – you will be surprised how different people can be.

As Alex came to the end of his science degree his dad began suggesting 'good jobs' for him to look at – things like accountancy or insurance work. Alex knew his dad meant well, but the sort of jobs he suggested depressed Alex deeply. He felt he was being pushed into drudgery.

Both Alex and his dad did the 'values' exercise. His dad's were money and security; Alex's (by a wide margin) was valuable work. They realised that each defined 'success' very differently. Alex eventually went into journalism – and loved it.

Other Personal Values

Other values may affect what sort of work you want to do.

 EXERCISE 3.3

Listed below are some contrasting values. Circle which word or phrase most appeals to you. If a category is unimportant to you, ignore it.

Predictability	Variety	Change
Anonymity	Recognition	High Profile
Tranquillity	Varied pace of work	Pressure
Working alone	Working alone and in a team	Team working
No competition	Some competition	Highly competitive
No fixed hours	Flexible working times	Defined hours
No clear promotion structure	Some promotion opportunities	Clearly defined promotion structure
No physical risk	Some physical risk	Physically risky
No emotional risk	Some emotional risk	Emotionally risky
Independence	Some guidance	Close direction or monitoring by others
Unhurried pace	Variable pace of work	Fast paced

Little challenge	Occasionally challenging	Very challenging – need to constantly adapt
Once trained, predictable	Sometimes have to learn new things	Constant learning
Responsible for no one	Leader of small team	Boss

Think about the categories you have marked. For example, if you prefer variety what do you mean by variety:

- frequently switching between different tasks?
- working in different locations?
- working with different people?
- something else? – What?

'Risk' and 'pressure', for example, mean different things to different people.

REFLECTION 3.3

- Are any of these very strong preferences or aversions? If so, note them.
- Do you think you have marked any because you have little experience of the area and are uncertain of yourself (for example, being in charge of others or being able to handle pressure)? If so it is worth bearing in mind that this is just an area where you have had little experience.

Remember that few people find a perfect job that fits every personal preference, and that being forced to work outside your own 'comfort zone' is challenging and sometimes, in the long run, enriching.

Values and career choice

Your values in themselves do not necessarily indicate a preference for a specific job, but they may help you to work out why some jobs appeal more than others. (For example, many Vs will be found in education, and few Ms in religious ministry.) It is important to keep your values in mind and ask yourself if the type of work you are considering will fulfil them:

- What are your key (and other) values?
- What might this mean in terms of the job you do?
- Or the type of organization you want to work for?
- Or the working conditions you would prefer?

Your values may influence what type of employer you want to work for (or whether to be self-employed): someone with 'prestige' as a motivator may want to work for a well known company in preference to a smaller, less well known one – even though the job and conditions may be similar. Someone valuing 'security' might want to work for an established organization even though a newer one might pay better. A 'valuable work' (V) accountant may hate his work with a chemical company – but love a similar job in the public sector.

You might consider the aims of the organization – to make a profit, provide a service, further a cause etc. (see Chapter 5); or the way it is structured ('independents' and 'imaginatives' may well hate bureaucracies). Or working conditions ('friendships' are unlikely to enjoy being isolated in their work).

New ways of working and changes in society may profoundly affect people whose values are threatened. For example, people working in public service jobs may lose satisfaction if the organization they work for is privatized and becomes geared to profit-making. Keep your values in mind throughout your working life and you'll know why you are feeling happy or dissatisfied with your job.

Summary

- A job that fulfils your key values will energize you, but a job that doesn't fulfil them will demotivate you.
- Note what *you personally* would look for in a fulfilling job.
- Are there implications for the types of jobs or employers you might be looking for?

Your skills

You will have seen from Chapter 2 that many graduate jobs ask for graduates in 'any discipline'. If the actual subject-related knowledge you gained from your degree isn't always important, what other things can you offer a potential employer?

This part of the chapter is intended to:

- Help you articulate the skills you have (essential when making applications for jobs).
- Help you in identifying types of work you might enjoy.
- Boost your confidence.

It is long and with many exercises. And, it is important. Please do take your time over the exercises, as the more thoroughly you do them the more you will benefit.

REFLECTION 3.4

- How important is it for you to find work you enjoy?
- How much time and effort are you prepared to put in to get it?

What skills do you have?

EXERCISE 3.4

Jot down ten skills you think you have. (Don't worry about the precise definition of skill).
   Then write ten more.

> '*What do you think are the personal skills and qualities that make you suited for the National Health Service Management Training Scheme?*'
>   (Question from a past NHS graduate application form)

Please read on only after you have finished Exercise 3.4.

Could you easily come up with 20 skills? Could you have written 40? Or did you struggle? Most students and graduates I have worked with can't easily say what skills they have. They are skilled, but are unaware of it. (So how are they going to persuade an employer to hire them?) Many people under-estimate their skills for a variety of reasons:

- They don't want to boast.
- They think everyone has the skills they have.
- They are genuinely unaware of what they can do.

Increasing Skills Awareness

Let's look for a moment at baby-sitting: a job many people will have done. What might be involved?

- Changing nappies
- Preparing food
- Making the child comfortable / giving reassurance
- Being firm when necessary
- Enforcing rules
- Being persuasive
- Reassuring parents
- Listening to the child/parents
- Thinking of strategies, e.g. if the child won't sleep
- Inventing games
- Understanding and remembering instructions

Note that the skills involved include working with things, people, ideas and information, although the 'people' skills predominate. Classifying skills in this way can give you pointers to the work you might enjoy, as different jobs may involve different types of skills (compare, for example, nursing and accountancy).

Or think of someone whose hobby is sailing. They may have manual, navigation and team-working skills (all of which we could break down further).

 REFLECTION 3.5

Does this approach seem over the top? Is it going too far to describe the skills used for a simple job? People tend to think things are easy once they have mastered the skills involved (driving a car, for example).

The next exercise is to alert you to the skills you have and to help you to think about those you most enjoy using. You may be surprised by some of the things in the list below.

Identifying your skills

 EXERCISE 3.5

Look at the list of skills below. Highlight those you think you are good at (compared with most people – you are not claiming to be an expert).

Researching information
Using tools
Using technical instruments
Encouraging people
Managing your time
Repairing things
Keeping records

Precision work with your hands
Playing an instrument
Composing music
Seeing solutions to problems
Seeing new possibilities
Expressing yourself through words
Using your imagination
Observing clearly
Remembering accurately
Driving a car or motorcycle
Making things
Keeping fit
Listening carefully
Organizing information
Making things grow
Persuading
Remembering details
Drawing
Making clothes
Defusing confrontations or quarrels
Leading or encouraging others
Showing enterprise

Working with numbers
Being physically coordinated
Devising games or exercises
Mental arithmetic
Following instructions
Quick physical reactions
Performing in front of an audience
Giving a presentation
Communicating through speech
Showing empathy, warmth
Communicating through writing
Using machinery (e.g. lathe, sewing machine)
Using shapes and colours
Explaining something clearly
Solving problems
Coaching
Managing money
Adapting things or ideas
Analysing information
Negotiating
Improvising
Getting on with different people
Building things
Enduring physical difficulties
Monitoring procedures
Mathematical skills
Organizing or classifying information

Writing a report	Using statistics
Using humour	Speaking clearly
Meeting deadlines	Thinking logically
Working with others	Evaluating/appraising
Using spreadsheets	Designing an experiment
Initiating/starting something up	Playing a sport
Word-processing	Acting
Speaking a language	Interpreting a plan or diagram

Note that many items can be further broken down: 'giving presenta-tions', for example, might include a range of skills from the technical (using PowerPoint) to 'people' skills (estimating the needs of the audience).

Adding to your skills list

EXERCISE 3.6

The list above is only a taster of possible skills. Now you need to add other skills which you have but which are not on the list above. (Note that we usually think of skills in terms of action verbs – *reassuring* people, *mending* motorbikes) You will certainly have other skills. For example:

1 Skills *specific to your degree subject* (For example, using a database, using scientific equipment, identifying dialects, being non-judgmental . . . Or your course may have provided a specific Learning Outcomes list in the course handbook or website.) Note them down now.
2 Skills you have *gained from jobs* – paid or unpaid (For example, using a till, stock control, keeping a child amused . . .)
3 Skills gained from *hobbies or leisure activities* (scuba-diving, drawing, first aid, map reading, basic mechanics . . .)

> *My hobbies are skills I never knew I had.*
>
> (Annabel)

4 Many university courses are specifically designed to develop certain *key skills* such as:

- *Communicating:* listening; explaining; debating; making presentations; writing essays; reports, learning journals; persuading, etc.
- *Working with others:* negotiating; delegating; taking responsibility; leading; cooperating; following instructions; defusing tensions . . .
- *Managing and organizing:* yourself; your time; meeting deadlines; planning your workload; using resources; researching and evaluating information . . .
- *Mathematical skills and numeracy:* including using statistics
- *IT:* spreadsheets; databases; word-processing; visual imaging; using web design; researching on-line . . .
- *Problem-solving:* analysing the problem; collecting information; devising solutions; evaluating strategies . . .

Note them down now.

It's a good idea to use your family and friends as 'sounding boards' – ask them if they think you are good at the same things *you* think you are good at. Often they can identify things you do well which you never realized. (Things that are easy or 'natural' to us we often think – wrongly – are natural to everyone else as well.) Or you could be deluding yourself about some perceived skills. Use this feedback to add to, or amend, your skills list.

> *Asking other people what they thought I could do was very eye-opening.*
>
> (James, final year undergraduate)

> *I believed I had no skills . . . after this exercise I began to realize I had many . . . some were gained through unpaid and unrecognized work. I had not appreciated their value . . . Now my list is embarrassingly long – from someone who thought they could not do anything.*
>
> (Kieran)

Keep adding to your list of skills whenever they occur to you.

Prioritising your skills

EXERCISE 3.7

Look back at your list of skills: mark the skills you would most like to use. This is especially useful in analysing what sort of job you might like. Note the skills you would like to use in paid work.

REFLECTION 3.6

There may be skills which you would like to use but not in your paid work, e.g. playing an instrument. If these are important to you, make sure you find an outlet for them – remember a life is not just made up of paid work!

Using skills as job indicators

Getting clues from your skills

Some careers theorists have postulated that people's skills cluster into certain areas, often given as:

1 **People**: If you have predominantly people skills you probably will enjoy working with people, but you need to think of how: e.g. *helping, teaching, selling to, instructing, motivating, entertaining, persuading.* Which most appeals to you? Appropriate fields of work could include social services, medicine, education, sales, and management.

2 **Ideas**: Ideas people like abstract thinking, making mental models, putting concepts together, being creative, discovering, interpreting: with *words, music* or *figures*. Fields of activity could include the arts, social sciences, law and scientific investigation.

3 **Things**: If you have lots of 'things' skills you probably like *materials, machines, instruments* or *growing things*. People with 'things' skills like to make, build, repair, invent. They might work in engineering, construction, maintenance, transport, agriculture or horticulture.

4 **Data/Information**: People with these skills like to organize, communicate or assess information in *words* or *figures*, etc. People with these skills often enjoy *systems* and *routines*. Fields of work could

include administration, finance, information systems, computers and libraries.

These classifications are rather crude, and many jobs employ a range of skills. However, they could give you a start in thinking about career options.

 REFLECTION 3.7

- Do they match with any ideas or preferences you have already?
- Brainstorm – what fields of work might utilise these skills? Ask other people for ideas.

 EXERCISE 3.8

Look at the list of skills you said you wanted to use in paid work.

- Can you classify them in any of the above four areas (people, things, data, ideas)?
- Do they 'cluster' into any one or two areas? Does this feel right to you?

The words in italics in the four areas may also be useful as a source of clues to things you might look for in a job. Note any that strike you as important.

Giving evidence of your skills

This evidence will be invaluable when you come to make applications.

 EXERCISE 3.9

Choose two or three of the skills you want to use in paid work. What *evidence* would you give to prove that you have them (i.e. in what situations have you used these skills)? You can use any area of your life:

- University courses
- Jobs (paid or unpaid)
- Hobbies or leisure activities (e.g. clubs, travel, music, Duke of Edinburgh's Award)
- Life generally (e.g. bringing up children, special achievements, difficulties overcome)

In most courses I have had to give oral presentations. I feel from this I have gained greater communication skills – thinking of what to say that would interest the audience, using visual aids to make it more lively, how to fit it into 15 minutes, plus forming and presenting arguments clearly.

(From a student's job application form).

Building on skills

A skill used in one context might be used or adapted for others. For example, the skills of listening with careful attention might be used by:

- An Occupational Therapist working with a patient
- A teacher listening to a pupil or parent
- A good friend 'being there' for someone
- A systems analyst finding out what the client wants the computer system to do
- An architect listening to what exactly the client needs

A skill gives you competence wherever you choose to use it.

Of course there are different levels of skills. For example there is a different level (and combination) of skills used in mechanics/engineering to: change a car tyre; change spark plugs; fit a new clutch; modify an engine; build an engine; design a new car. The same is true in teaching where you could be devising: games to amuse a child; a lesson to teach a class; a course or module; a scheme of study for a whole year group; a complete course of study spread over several years.

People usually develop their skills and competencies in stages (not always equal stages – we're sometimes thrown in at the deep end!). You can develop your skills by:

- being prepared to have a go
- making mistakes, reflecting and learning from them.

REFLECTION 3.8

How could you develop the skills you most want to use in work?
    Usually, the higher your levels of skill, the more freedom you have in your job.

Talents

A short word about talents. Some people have a talent for something that is so important to them that they become unhappy if they have no outlet for it.

- Do you have a burning talent?
- What do you really enjoy doing?
- What makes you lose all track of time?
- What makes your heart lift?

REFLECTION 3.9

How could you use this talent? In paid or unpaid activities? How might you build it into your life?

Summary

- You should now be able to articulate at least some of your skills and give evidence to prove you have them.
- You should be clearer about the ones you ideally do (and don't) want to use in paid work.
- Skills learned in one context can be used in others.
- You should build on skills, or use sets of skills to develop your competencies.

> *This exercise has enabled me to say that I'm good at some things and can actually do the job I previously believed was beyond my abilities. Initially I floundered at being asked about my skills – now it's a case of, How long have you got?*
>
> (Third year undergraduate)

Your personality

Often personality traits are as important to employers as the skills a likely candidate has. Some jobs require particular temperaments – you might want a powerful, decisive personality as prime minister, for example, but the same person may not have the sensitivity and empathy to nurse the dying.

Some employers, when advertising vacancies, clearly have certain personality types in mind. Revenue and Customs, in its ads for tax inspectors, emphasizes skills in solving puzzles, crosswords and jig-saws – not because doing these are part of the job (!) but because a liking for them indicates the sort of meticulous, logical, analytical mind that the job requires.

Of course, our personality is affected by many things – our values, skills, experiences etc. In this part of the chapter I'll mention a few aspects of personality which may help you identify jobs you might enjoy.

Different 'intelligences'

Have you ever been hopeless at a job or task? Have you been given something simple to do and failed? It's easy to think, 'I must be stupid' and feel worthless, but it may just be that you haven't developed that type of 'intelligence'.

Different people have different intelligences (and different combinations of intelligences). You can be a beautiful writer, but be quite incapable of making toast without burning it; you could be a successful scientist but be hopeless with your kids; you could be a marvellous dancer, but unable to add up your cheque book.

Here are some possible 'intelligences' (with key words linked to each) – do any of them apply to you?

- Artistic (self-expression, feelings, creativity)
- Mathematical (numbers, algebra, chess, logic, strategy, science)
- Body (dance, coordination, sport, building and repairing, being practical)
- Social (sensitive to moods, good listener, good mixer)
- Personal (meditative, using intuition, personal development, spirituality)
- Spatial (plans, diagrams, layouts, maps, sculptures)
- Language (words, jokes, aesthetics of words – e.g. poetry – rhythm, rhyme)
- Linguistic (foreign languages, phonetics, grammar, dialects)
- Musical (playing an instrument, reading music, singing, composing)
- Visual (sensitive to shape, colour, line, form, design)
- Practical (making, mending, growing things)

REFLECTION 3.10

What implications might these have for possible job choices?

Thinking about your personality

It's often difficult to be accurate about our personality traits because we're rarely objective about ourselves, and because of the old story – the capacities that are second nature to us, we think everyone has.

Rowena was always the person people confided in. She was honest, sensible, kind and never gossiped. Even her tutor discussed his problems with her! Rowena never grasped that this was unusual or important. After many years of working in a lab she finally discovered her vocation – as a counsellor. Most of her friends could have suggested this years before.

EXERCISE 3.10

Note down some aspects of your personality, and ask others what they think. (It is important to get feedback from others, for this section in particular.) Here are some words suggesting personality traits – make a note of any you think you have (and those you definitely don't have!):

leader	timid	self-confident	decisive
strict honesty	empathy for others	motivates	quick thinking
cheerful	persistent	resilient	common sense
makes things happen	sees possibilities	imaginative	realistic
forceful	enthusiastic	assertive	dominant
shrinking	tactful	persuasive	hard-working
creative	shy	fair	compliant
open-minded	follows rules	go-getting	energetic
responsible	disciplined	kind	approachable
gregarious	adaptable	builds relationships	committed
efficient	disorganized	self-aware	authoritative
reliable	ambitious	takes the initiative	(add others)

Note that opposite qualities to some of these are also important. No value judgement is necessarily implied: for example, one job may need people who follow rules and procedures carefully; another may want creative types who always look for new ways of doing things.

Think about these personality traits: how might some aspects of your personality affect your job choice? For example:

- If you enjoy or hate risk?
- Enjoy or hate rules and procedures?
- Are good at inspiring people?
- Are a self-starter or prefer to be guided?
- Are shy or outgoing?

Are there any aspects you need to work on?

Personality in career choice

Careers theorist John Holland has pioneered the relationship between people's personality and the work they may feel comfortable doing. He identified six broad personality types and related work environments. The types are:

1 *Social:* Enjoy working with people and using feelings and intuition. They like to help others: educating, healing, supporting. They might enjoy things like teaching, nursing, social work, therapies.
2 *Enterprising:* Also like working with people, but with the emphasis on leading, persuading and managing. Often they are confident

risk-takers. They can be found in areas like politics, business management and sales.

3 *Realistic:* Like working with their hands, tools, machines or practical
things. Often enjoy working alone or outdoors. They like concrete
problems and practical solutions. They would include farmers,
gardeners, surveyors, plumbers, electricians, engineers, pilots.

4 *Artistic:* Like to make their own solutions, do things differently, use
their imaginations. Creative, often introspective and unconventional,
they typically enjoy things like art, music, dance, drama, writing,
design, architecture. They often value unstructured work environments, situations where they can express themselves. Obviously
found in the arts and creative industries, such as architecture, design
and writing.

5 *Conventional:* Like order, organization and routine. They enjoy using
logic and tend to be good with data, information, detail and responsibility. Often the backbone of organizations, conventional types like
following systems and routines and would be comfortable with order
and hierarchy. Typical jobs might be clerical, administrative, banking,
taxation, data-handling.

6 *Investigative:* Like using their ideas, curiosity and intellect to solve
problems. They analyse, observe, theorize and can be very task
orientated. Enjoy independence; often introspective and unconventional. Typically found in the sciences, maths, medicine.

Remember that 'types' are to be used as tools, not labels: people
don't usually fit neatly into one type or another – we tend to blend
and blur, using different aspects of ourselves, with some aspects being
predominant. Holland's types are guidelines to give you clues about
your job preferences. You can find your 'type' in more detail by
doing Holland's Self Directed Search available at www.self-directed-
search.com

Of all Holland's 'types' it's usually the artistic people who find it difficult to relate to work opportunities. Unless you're very talented and
have a vocation, it's difficult to see what outlet there might be for your
talents. In fact there are many possibilities, especially if you bear in mind
that jobs tend to be made up of different elements, and there may well be
scope for your creativity in at least some aspect of many jobs. Artistic
types often have to research opportunities more carefully than other
groups – be prepared to use your creative talents in your job-hunting!
(See also Further Information for some pointers in this).

Another personality guide you may find useful is the Myers-Briggs
Type Inventory (MBTI) which is often used in training courses. Your

Careers Service may run MBTI sessions, or you can find information in Myers and Myers (1993) *Gifts Differing* (see Further information).

Your interests

This section will look at what you enjoy spending time on, to help you:

- Become aware of how much knowledge you have in a variety of different areas (you never know when this may come in useful).
- Reflect upon whether your interests might influence the fields of work you would enjoy.
- Start thinking about how your interests contribute to your happiness, and whether you need to build them into your life in work or leisure time.

> Julian got a job with wool importers. During the interview he impressed them with his knowledge – gained in his gap year on an Australian sheep farm!

What do you know about?

 EXERCISE 3.11

Jot down as many of your areas of knowledge that you can think of (you don't have to be an expert in the area). Here are a few ideas to get you going:

football	singing	playing the flute	statistics
child-care	computer	astronomy	modern dance
teenagers	programming	railways	gardens
cooking	bereavement	fashion	auditing
how people learn	horses	motorbikes	hang-gliding
scuba-diving	religion	plumbing	Russian
training dogs	navigation	the Scout	Literature
film	interior design	movement	chemistry

Now make your own list.

> Suzanne got a research post with an environmental organization because they valued her scuba diving qualifications as well as her degree.

 REFLECTION 3.11

What articles do you read first in the newspaper or magazines? What *issues* are important to you? Jot them down. Would you like to use or develop these fields of knowledge:

- in paid work?
- in unpaid work?
- in leisure activities?

Interests in career choice

Having a job connected to one of your interests can make all the difference. Someone passionate about horses, for example, might enjoy selling equine supplies, whereas they might not enjoy selling confectionery. You often find sailing or surfing enthusiasts working in supply shops, or anywhere where they can mix with fellow enthusiasts. In this case, the interest is so all-consuming that the type of job is secondary.

The word 'hobby' rather implies something unimportant, used just to fill spare time. However hobbies can be very important to some people – look at the painter, L.S. Lowry – he collected rents for a living but painting was more important to him. Some climbers take short-term jobs where the job is relatively unimportant – the goal is to amass enough money for the next expedition. Remember that different people have different career paths.

However interests can sometimes, in my experience, be red-herrings. Many graduates are passionate about music and some assume that this means their dream job would be in the music industry. This isn't always the case. A job is always a blend of different elements and sometimes the context of the job doesn't compensate for other aspects.

Phil, a second year undergraduate, was desperate to arrange a place-ment with the A & R (Artist and Repertoire) department of a record company. It took a huge amount of effort and perseverance, but he managed to get one. He found that he hated it. He saw the music industry was just that – an industry.

After months of effort Tom arranged his dream placement with a football club, but at the last minute they pulled out. He was devastated and took whatever he could get – a placement in the HQ of a large brewing com-pany, helping to compile the annual report. He loved every minute; especially the camaraderie as the team worked towards a tight deadline.

REFLECTION 3.12

A career isn't just about jobs, it's a 'path through life'. Do reflect upon what you want in your life:

- What do you really enjoy doing?
- What makes your heart lift?
- What makes you lose all track of time?
- How can you build this into your life (in work or leisure)?

Your personal preferences

There now follows a selection of exercises looking at different personal preferences, particularly in relation to paid work. Some may be useful to you, others may not, but note any that are and don't worry about those that aren't. (Although sometimes it may be useful to note things that you definitely *don't* want in your work.)

People you would enjoy working with

 EXERCISE 3.12

1 What kind of people would you like to work with? Note any preferences from any of these categories of people you might want to work *for* or *alongside*, as colleagues.

children (ages?)	poor people	rich people	highly intelligent people
disabled people	elderly	adolescents	people of a different religion or culture
different races	mentally ill	prisoners	musicians
babies	adults	slow learners	witnesses
the military	boys	girls	sports people
women	men	retired people	(other)
physically ill people	people my age	the general public	

2 Would you like to be with them as:

- customers?
- clients?
- colleagues?
- students?
- other?

3 Looking at the types of people you might want to work with, not as colleagues but as clients, etc. (for example, elderly people), would you like to be:

- helping them?
- counselling them?
- persuading them?
- selling to them?
- supporting them?
- teaching them?
- (other).

4 And is your preferred way to work:

- alone?
- in a small group?
- in a large team?
- with different people at different times?
- (other).

Things you would enjoy working with

 EXERCISE 3.13

Are there any types of things you enjoy being with or using? For example:

machines	textiles	boats	stationery
colours	aircraft	plants	food
toys	books	cars	sports equipment
computers	furniture	clothes	scientific instruments
paintings	flip charts	pens	musical instruments
sculptures	manuals	tools	recording equipment
cameras	calculators	engines	maps
(other)			

Note them down, being as specific as possible. Do any have implications for the work you want to do or the environment you might feel happiest in (an office, a studio, a workshop, a library, a laboratory)?

Rosie always loved stationery, pens, blackboards, flipcharts and a classroom environment . . . but she thought she didn't want to teach . . . until she realized that 'teaching' needn't just mean school-teaching, or teaching youngsters. She joined a consultancy group, training business managers.

Work places you would enjoy working in

 EXERCISE 3.14

What kind of workplace do you think you would most enjoy?

big office full of people	farm	factory floor	ship
small office	residential home	shop	sports centre
working outdoors (in all weathers?)	hospital	café/restaurant	community centre
laboratory	on the road (travelling)	kitchen	clients' homes
workshop	at home	studio	classroom
(other)			

(You may ideally like a job which combines some of these, e.g. on the road but with an office base.)

> Annette enjoys being a farm secretary because it enables her to live and work in the countryside, without the need for lengthy commuting.

Do you have experience of any/many of these work places? Are you making assumptions which have not been tested? For example, many students say, 'I don't want to work in an office', which might mean:

- I don't want to be told what to do.
- I don't want to be faceless.
- I want to do something useful, not 'push paper'.
- I don't like filing.
- I don't like administration.
- My holiday job was so boring . . .
- I don't want to work 9–5.

> *I always said I never wanted to work in an office. I've been doing it for two years now. And I love it. I love having an office – I can shut the door!*
> (Julie)

Where do you think you would like to work? Or do you have no preferences?

Where do you want to live?

EXERCISE 3.15

Where would you like to live?

- In a city where things are happening
- In the countryside
- Abroad (where?)
- Near my partner
- Staying put where I live now
- Close to e.g. climbing or sailing facilities
- Near my family

For some people, where they live is of especial importance. For example, you may want to be near your partner or you may not want to uproot the kids. The psychologist, Carl Jung, needed to live near water; Emily Bronte was incapacitated by homesickness when she left Haworth. For many these might be quite minor considerations, for others they might be crucial to their well-being.

Some graduates' career choice is dictated by geography – needing to find work where their partner is, for example. In this case, it is often useful to think, not in terms of a place ('I need to work in York') but, how much time you are willing to give to travelling to work. If you research travelling times and transport options, then you should get a radius of places where you might feasibly look for work.

REFLECTION 3.13

Is there any aspect of your life that is really important to you? Or that you would like to have if possible (e.g. you might like to work in your home town eventually, but realize that you might need to work away for a few years first . . .)?

Do you want to make a contribution to the world in some way?

EXERCISE 3.16

What would you like your work, ideally, to contribute to the world?

persuades people	promotes change	transports things
sells a product	exploits natural resources	repairs things
invents something	provides a service	recycles things
helps people	promotes justice	builds something
produces goods	realises a vision	starts something (what?)
increases knowledge	protects something	creates beauty
promotes something	creates jobs	entertains people
teaches something	creates wealth	(other)

Elaborate on any of these that are important to you e.g. teach whom? protect what?

Another way to approach this question is to ask yourself: what do you find yourself thinking about?

- Do you mentally put the world right?
- Designing something?
- Planning something?
- Persuading someone?
- Explaining something?
- Driving something forward?
- (other)

What might this indicate?

Other points to think about

REFLECTION 3.14

Remember that I'm defining a career as a 'path through life'. Getting paid work that you enjoy will be important, but it is only a part of your life. We have already seen that things like hobbies can also contribute to people's well-being, as can other considerations (e.g. wanting to pay off student debts, wanting a family, pets, or the chance to travel).

- Are there any other things you would like to note as being important to you in the long- or short-term?
- Are there any other areas you would like to look at which might illuminate your career preferences?

Putting it all together

You now have a great quantity of information. You have examined your personal skills, values, interests, aspects of your personality and personal preferences – all of which may have implications for what type of work you might or might not enjoy. This part of the chapter is to encourage you to gather this information to produce a 'template' which you can use in evaluating job opportunities.

A portrait of you

 EXERCISE 3.17

1 Take a large sheet of paper. In the centre put a picture of anything which makes you happy e.g. a photograph, postcard or cutting – as long as it's something which *lifts your spirits* when you look at it. (This is to motivate and inspire you. If the whole idea of making a 'career choice' makes you anxious, use something that makes you smile.)
2 Around the picture write out the results of the exercises in each part of this section. Also include important details – this paper will be your record and guide to what you are looking for in a job. Please do this as thoroughly as you can.

   - Your *key values*
   - Other important *values*
   - The *skills* you most enjoy using
   - Aspects of your *personality*
   - Any *fields of knowledge* you would ideally like to use in your work
   - The *people* you would like to work with and how you want to work with them (e.g. as clients, patients, students . . .)

- The *things* you enjoy working with
- The *contribution* you want to make

Plus any of these which seem useful:

- Your preferred working *environment*
- The *place(s)* you hope to work in
- Any *other* consideration

3 Highlight items that are of *high priority* to you (e.g. your key values, or the town you need to live in, etc.)
4 Try to summarize your personal record. An example summary might be:

> *It's important to me to use my work to make friendships. I should like to work with a team or small group of people, and I enjoy helping or teaching people. I especially like to be with people who are physically disabled or adolescents. I am reliable, responsible and well organized. I am good at encouraging people, providing a supportive and sympathetic environment, drawing people out. I am quite creative and like to use my imagination to devise new ways of doing things . . .*

 REFLECTION 3.15

What ideas are occurring to you, about areas of employment which might incorporate at least some of your preferences? The person in point 4 of Exercise 3.17, for example, might decide to start by investigating careers in medical-related therapies or in teaching special needs youngsters, or in some type of social work . . .

Do discuss your page of information with your family and friends. They could provide feedback on its accuracy and give you ideas about what it suggests.

Think about the following questions and points:

- What do you really enjoy doing?
- What makes your heart lift?
- What makes you lose all track of time?

- How could you build this into your life (in work or leisure)?
- Try to be aware of what energizes and what crushes you.

Using this information to choose job areas to investigate

We saw at the start of this chapter ('Choosing a career') that a common model of career choice requires you to do a self-inventory of your skills, values, etc., which you have now done. You should now have a much clearer idea of what you are looking for in your ideal work, and what you can offer employers. You can use this information as a 'template' with which to evaluate any opportunities that arise. It should also be useful in giving guidance about possible areas of work to investigate further. (Do take this with you if you book an appointment with a careers adviser.)

As you completed each section, you may well have been getting clearer ideas about possible jobs or employment sectors or, at least, things to avoid. It may have been confirming ideas you already had.

But, as I have mentioned before, don't get too hung up on job titles. You don't have to say, 'I want to be a . . .' to be effective in your job-hunting.

Here is an alternative model of career choice:

 REFLECTION 3.16

Imagine you are going to the Sales. You don't know what will be available, what has already been snapped up or what is more than you can afford. So you might put together a shopping list. Say you want a winter coat:

- Does it have to be a coat? Can it be a jacket? What length?
- Is it to be in this season's fashion or in a style to last?
- Is it for work or leisure?
- Is it for warmth or style?
- Should it be patterned or plain?
- What colour, size, style should it be?

You might have a very good idea of what you want and be lucky enough to find it. But what if you can't find it? Or it's too expensive? You see other possibilities – but are any of them worth buying?

If you have a clear idea of what you want, e.g. 'I want a coat for warmth that will last, that will ideally be navy but I'll look at other colours, that will ideally be knee-length and won't cost more than £X . . .', then you can be open to the opportunities available without falling for something completely unsuitable. In other words, if you know what you want, and what you can compromise on, then you can take advantage of the opportunities available.

Similarly, you might have an idea of your ideal job. But these jobs may be scarce and perhaps you are limited by geography or because you don't yet have all the qualifications or experience you would need. If you have a good idea of *what you can offer* and *what you would enjoy* and are prepared to have a go at something new, then you will be able to make the most of what is available.

Getting help

This would be a good time to use your university careers service, either by browsing in the careers library or, armed with your page of self-information, by discussing options with a careers adviser. Used intelligently, your university careers service is a truly invaluable resource. However, students often have a naive idea of what a careers adviser can do: sometimes they expect careers advisers, after a half-hour interview, to tell them 'what to be'. Careers advisers have knowledge and expertise but not second sight!

You may want to try a computer program like Prospects Planner to help you match your preferences to possible job areas. Prospects Planner is available on the Prospects website (www.prospects.ac.uk) or, in a fuller version, at your university careers service. Use this intelligently though – as a guide to where you might start your investigations, not as a crystal ball telling you to 'be an X'. Computer programs, however sophisticated, have a relatively limited database of job titles – and we have seen how unhelpful it can be to fixate on a job title.

Summary

You now have a detailed snapshot of yourself at this point in your life. You can use this to:

- give you ideas about job areas you might investigate, and
- as a 'template' to evaluate any opportunities that might come up.

4

Researching opportunities

Starting your research • Researching an occupation • Information interviews • Making the most of a work placement • Researching other options • How do people find jobs? • Summary

Chapter 3 gave you some possible starting points for jobs you might like to investigate. In Chapter 4 we look at how to find out more about those jobs. This chapter will help you in deciding what types of jobs you might enjoy and should improve your chances of getting one.

You can use the techniques you learn from this section to investigate all sorts of different opportunities, not just for job-hunting. If you're contemplating postgraduate study you could research course options and (if the course is vocational) whether the extra qualification will help you to get the job you want. If you're thinking of travelling and working overseas, you can investigate possible routes and strategies to fund your travels. If you hope to be self-employed, you could use the techniques given here to direct your research to starting up your own business. Mostly, however, this section will look at researching an occupation and how people get jobs.

We have seen how quickly jobs and the workplace are changing, and how it is predicted that graduates may have to face numerous (voluntary or involuntary) job changes throughout their working lives. To cope with this, graduates need to develop career management skills, including being able to research the opportunities open to them. Techniques learned here can be used to investigate these opportunities and to make effective applications throughout your working life, not just immediately after graduation.

Starting your research

As an undergraduate you will have spent hours and hours researching information for reports, essays, dissertations, etc. You now need to use these skills in researching your career options. If you research a job you can gain invaluable information such as:

- whether it's the sort of job you want to do
- whether there are similar jobs you haven't thought of
- how people get these jobs
- how to make the best possible applications

Don't dismiss your dreams

Some people dismiss as fantasy or 'pie in the sky' jobs they secretly cherish. They're afraid of being 'unrealistic' or think they have no chance, so don't even try to get the job of their dreams. I would always encourage you to check out whether your ideas really are fantasy or not. People do get their dream jobs! Don't be put off by people talking about 'the real world' – a deadening (and meaningless) phrase. If you have a passion or dream – go for it. If it doesn't work out, then adapt. But don't give up before you even start. One key element in achieving a goal, or realizing a dream, is to *believe that it is possible* – then you will put real effort into it.

Start by finding out if your dream job exists or is feasible for you right now. If you research the job thoroughly you can gain invaluable information – including whether you want the job at all. By investigating the job you could also get ideas about other options, and find out about ways in – people often get jobs in unusual ways.

A good test as to whether a job is fantasy or something you would really want to do, is to ask yourself *how much time and effort are you prepared to put into getting it?* If you aren't prepared to spend time or effort or to take a risk (for example, risking rejection) it suggests that, underneath, you might not want the job after all. (If this is your conclusion, think about what aspect of the dream job is important to you. Is there any way you can build this into your life, even if it isn't your bread-and-butter work?)

I had two students who wanted to work in film. John said confidently that he 'wanted to direct'. Mira wasn't sure, but she loved the medium. I suggested to both that they could start their investigations by talking to people at our local film archive: not difficult, as it was based on campus. Mira did an information interview [which we look at later] with the director of the archive and ended up with a voluntary job where she learned about the medium, film restoration and the basics of editing. She also joined the local film society and became their student rep. After graduating she got a place on a very competitive MA and is now working in film. John never even approached the archive. I think his might have been a 'fantasy' job which, in his heart, he didn't really want.

   Don't be too proud to look for alternative ways into competitive jobs: remember all the film directors who started out making the tea!

Think creatively about your options. (One writer I met took an early morning cleaning job to give herself time to write plays during the day.) Some students want to write – all you need is pen, paper and an hour a day. If you're an aspiring film-maker all you need is to get your hands on a digital camera . . . Sometimes dreams become reality in unlikely ways, or after taking circuitous routes – but if something is important to you, pursue it.

Don't dismiss your dreams – investigate them!

Lorna was an unemployed graduate who confessed during a careers interview that actually, what she would love to do would be to design and decorate cakes. I asked her how much equipment she needed. 'Oh,' she said, 'I've got it.' So, I asked *why aren't you making cakes now?*

Researching an occupation

Questions to ask

Your first task is to work out what exactly you need to find out. If you are researching a job to see whether it's something you would want to do, the personal portrait you compiled in Chapter 3, 'Putting it all together' (pp. 51–53) is the best starting point (i.e., does this job match your *values*; does it involve *skills* you enjoy using; does it match any or most of your *preferences*, etc.)

If you are fairly certain this is a job you want to do, you may want to investigate other things – best employers, promotion prospects, etc.

Here are some typical things to find out:

- What the job involves day to day
- What the working conditions are like (e.g. hours, physical environment)
- What skills are required
- What qualifications are essential or useful
- What experience (if any) is looked for
- How people get this job (Where are vacancies advertised? Are they ever advertised?). If it's very competitive, are there 'back doors' into the job?
- What prospects are there?
- What requirements are there (e.g. dress codes, confidentiality agreements, etc.)?
- Would you have to travel; move house often, etc.?
- Would you be required to do further professional training?
- Which organizations employ people in this job?
- Is it a growth area or are jobs hard to find?
- What makes someone good at this job?

 EXERCISE 4.1

Develop your own list of things you *personally* want to find out about a possible job. Prioritize them.

Some things you may be able to ask directly, such as: 'Would I have to be highly numerate?' Other things, especially value-related information, such as, 'Would this fulfil my need to do something valuable for its own sake?' may be a matter of judgement after you have obtained as much information as possible.

After researching an occupation, look at your personal portrait (see Chapter 3, 'Putting it all together' (pp. 51–53) and compare the job with it. There will rarely be a perfect fit, but a good correlation suggests this is a job you might enjoy.

Resources

Now you know *what* you want to find out, you need to think about how to go about getting the information.

Careers service

Your university or college careers service is an obvious resource. And you may be surprised by the very diverse information they have. Information on occupations will be classified so that similar jobs are grouped together – this may help you widen your ideas. They will also have many free brochures, e.g. AGCAS information booklets and GTI guides, some of which may contain information on types of careers in different sectors. Employers' recruitment literature may contain case histories of various jobs. The careers library will also have information on: postgraduate courses and financing them; working overseas; local employers; and self-employment.

Websites

www.prospects.ac.uk is a good place to start. It provides basic information on many types of jobs. Again, employer websites may contain job-related information.

Professional associations

Many occupations have professional associations, e.g. the Advertising Association, CILIP (Libraries), Chartered Institute of Management Accountants. Many produce careers information either as booklets or on their websites. The *Directory of British Associations* provides information on thousands of hugely diverse organizations.

Journals

Relevant professional journals can be useful in giving you a flavour of the world of a particular profession. For example, the *Bookseller* contains jobs and information on publishing; the *Times Education Supplement* will give you insight into issues affecting teachers; other specialist magazines such as the *Nursing Times* or the *Economist* will give you insight into different working areas. Find a relevant publication by consulting *Willings Press Guide* (in most academic libraries).

Careers advisers

Could help you clarify your ideas and may come up with other suggestions.

Books about the occupation

Can be variable in quality and go out of date very quickly. You might also look at general books about the topic, e.g. management textbooks.

Talks

Your careers service may have organized a programme of visiting speakers – check them out. Sometimes you may be able to attend general meetings run by professional associations – especially if you have joined as a student member.

Visit to an employer

Again, some careers services may organize visits to big employers or employers might have public open days (e.g. small breweries are sometimes open to the public). Do you have any contacts through whom you could arrange a visit?

People working in the sector

One of the very best ways of getting up-to-date information is by talking to someone actually doing the job. This is so important I have dedicated a section to it later in the chapter (see 'Information interviews', p. 63).

Work placement

A work placement is often the very best opportunity for researching a job (see below).

Evaluating careers information

Just as with research done during your course, you need to have an awareness of the reliability of different sources of information. Do use your judgement to evaluate what you are learning. Here are some things to watch out for:

- *Date* of publication. Is it way out of date? Is the information still reliable?
- *Who* produced it? Was it written to recruit people, or even to put people off if the profession is overcrowded or highly competitive? A professional association, for example, might concentrate on the favourable aspects of a job. If something was published by AGCAS (Association of Graduate Careers Advisory Services) it was probably written by careers advisers who would be impartial, but would not actually be doing the job.
- *What* was it produced for: to inform or to entertain? Was it intended for job-seekers or for 'general interest' (e.g. TV programmes and magazine articles where there might be a bias towards the more glamorous or entertaining aspects of a job).

> Many careers advisers have reported increased interest in forensic science as a result of glamorous TV programmes – most of which bear little resemblance to the actual 'real life' job. Even documentaries have to concentrate on the dramatic and exciting aspects of a job.
>
> Negative publicity has an effect too – a high profile vilification of a social worker, for example, can lead to a drop in applicants for social work.

- *Personal bias or misinformation.* If you're interviewing someone, bear in mind what stage of their career they are at: are they new and enthusiastic or a burnt-out case? Does the interviewee have his/her own agenda? (They might, for example, resent graduates because they themselves don't have a degree.) Do they have out of date ideas ('I got in this way 20 years ago so I assume it applies now . . .') Family and friends – even tutors – might have out of date ideas about jobs they left years ago. Careers advisers too, can vary in their knowledge. Use multiple sources to enable you to double-check information.

Information interviews

Information interviewing means talking to someone who is doing a job you're interested in. It's a key skill for successful job hunters and job changers (see pp. 74–76); it's a great way to get the best, most up to date information; and it can make all the difference to your success in getting the job you want. It's most useful to do this after you have completed your preliminary research (see earlier in this chapter).

Some students find information interviewing daunting, but it *really is worth doing.* Over the years students have told me how useful their interviews have been: in finding up-to-date information; in getting an idea of what potential employers will be looking for, and in making contacts (that have frequently led to voluntary or paid jobs, or work placements). Information interviewing will also help you see that an 'employer' or 'organization' means a body of people, not a faceless and rather intimidating concept.

Finding someone to interview

The first stage is to find someone to interview. Here are some strategies:

1 Use any *contacts* you have – your extended family and friends, including friends of friends; employers; tutors; ex-teachers; acquaintances from your part-time or vacation work; social club members; the careers service; your alumni association . . . *tell* people that you are trying to find someone who works in, e.g. advertising, midwifery, theatre design . . . and ask if they know someone who you might contact. (When doing this in seminars we can almost always find contacts for any type of job – just from class members' acquaintances.)

> I interviewed someone on the train (never stay quiet on a train – it's amazing what you find out). I got shown round [a large employer] and interviewed for a placement in marketing.
>
> (Sarah)

2 Is there anyone in your university doing this job? (Universities have finance officers, counsellors, librarians, administrators, PR and marketing departments, printers, Health & Safety officers . . .)

3 Employer directories (available in your careers service) will list large graduate employers and identify what sort of jobs they recruit for. For smaller employers you could try your local employer lists (in your careers library) or the *Yellow Pages* to identify organizations doing the kind of work you're interested in. If you don't have any contacts – at any level – within the organization, you could try ringing the switchboard to try to identify a suitable person to approach.

4 Professional associations may be able to help you, particularly if there are local branches.

5 One contact will lead to others. Don't think that you have to concentrate on 'important' people.

6 Small businesses and organizations can be just as useful as large ones. (Sometimes more so, as this is an expanding sector for graduate recruitment.)

Brainstorm – write out as many contacts as possible before you decide on whom to approach first.

> Susan and Joe wanted to work in theatre. Susan *'couldn't find anyone to talk to'* – Joe talked to people doing several different kinds of jobs in theatres within a 30 mile radius of campus. He also got himself a voluntary job selling programmes, which enabled him to make contacts . . .

Arranging an interview

Telephone, email or write a friendly letter explaining who you are and why you want to interview the person (for *information* about their job). Specify the amount of time you would like, e.g. 20 minutes, and make the letter short and business-like. Before contacting someone, especially on the phone, make sure you have all your questions sorted out. Make it clear that you are looking for information *not* a job.

You may be surprised how willing people are to talk about their work to someone who shows a genuine interest (i.e., has researched it beforehand).

> *I found that the interview was more helpful than any research I have done . . . it gave me real insight into what the job is really like on an everyday level . . . I was surprised how easy it was to get an interview as I*

imagined no-one would have time to talk to me, but I think that possibly they have been in the same position I am now. . . . if you ask politely enough and don't take up too much of their time, people are more than willing to talk . . . doing this exercise has given me confidence.

(Helen, interested in stage design)

At the interview

- Be on time.
- Be smart (you want to create an impression).
- Take a pen and notebook and your list of questions.
- Stick to the time you asked for. If your time is up say something like 'There's more I could ask, but we've had our agreed 20 minutes'. Interviewees are usually busy people, so sticking to your agreement is courteous, and it allows the interviewee to conclude the interview or give you more time.
- *Tip:* It's always useful also to ask if there is anyone else that you might speak to. In this way you will get a variety of information and will have started 'networking' – i.e., making contacts.

Managers have to be focussed. They will respect you if you are too.

(Graduate employer)

How to Interview

An interview is a structured communication: it has a purpose. Your purpose is to get the information you need. So:

1 Know what you want to find out. Have your list of questions and ask the important ones first.
2 Know how to ask questions. Here are two types of question you might use:
   - The *factual question:* What qualifications are needed for this job? How long does training usually take?
   - The *'open' question:* These are questions that can't be answered by just 'yes' or 'no'. They encourage the interviewee to open up and elaborate upon their answers. For example: Could you describe a typical day? Have you any advice on how I might improve my chances?

3 Be open and friendly. Use appropriate body language (see Chapter 5, 'Interviews').

> *Don't be afraid to ask,* 'Do you employ people like me?' *What sort of people do you employ?*
>
> (Graduate employer)

After the interview

Thank your interviewee, but also write to them afterwards thanking them again. (They might then remember you if something comes up.)

> *Always write a thank you letter – it's also a good idea after job interviews. We were very impressed by a candidate who wrote to us to thank us for the interview. We offered the candidate the job.*
>
> (Employer, publishing)

 EXERCISE 4.2

Practise interviewing with a friend. Even if you feel awkward, it's worth doing and will give you confidence. You might ask each other about your degree course, work you have done or even 'desert island discs' – just to get you practising listening and using open questions. This is good practice for being interviewed too.

Interviewing on the phone

Just as with face-to-face interviews:

- Have a notebook and pen ready.
- Note the name, number and position of the person you're speaking to and the organization they work for.
- Note the date and time.
- Organize all your papers before you call, including having your questions ready, just in case.
- Think about what you will say.

- Speak clearly, don't mumble or shout.
- Be concise and sound purposeful.
- Don't eat or drink.
- Be pleasant and polite.

> Joanne rang a national magazine to ask for the name of someone who might be prepared to meet for an information interview. She was put through to a journalist who said, 'interview me now'. Joanne was prepared and rattled off her questions so professionally that she was asked if she was interested in a work placement. She was!
>
> (Remember that Joanne had probably taken a few rejections in her stride before this happened.)

Some students love 'information interviewing' – others find it demanding. It is, however, really worth doing. If you are apprehensive, ask yourself *what are you risking* – rejection? Looking an idiot? And then motivate yourself by thinking *what you might gain* – the possibility of greatly improving your chances of getting the job you really want. How important is that to you?

Over the years students in my classes have been surprised how willing many people (sometimes very famous individuals) have been to give their time as an interviewee – in person, over the phone or in response to a well thought out, brief questionnaire.

> Morag wanted to be an actress. She decided, however, it would be useful to information interview a theatrical agent – to get an idea of their business and their point of view. Her interview – conducted by questionnaire and phone – was so successful the agent offered her the chance to 'shadow' him in his work for a week. After this week, he offered to come (a considerable journey) to see her in her next college production.

Making the most of a work placement

If you are reading this before you graduate, do make the most of any opportunity to do a work placement. (If you have graduated or are doing a course where there is no placement, could you arrange one for yourself? I have had students who have done evening or week-end placements.) A work placement can really be an invaluable experience.

> *Although I had a variety of part-time jobs . . .the work placement had a very different effect on me . . . I experienced the satisfaction work can bring, in terms of having a role that I see as demanding, constructive and the final outcomes rewarding.*
> (Katherine, second year student, after a placement with a local authority)

Although some undergraduates complain bitterly about having to do a placement, seeing it purely in terms of 'work experience', it is a really great opportunity to investigate a job you're interested in, to beef up your CV with relevant experience, and to give you confidence.

It can be *especially* useful for mature students, as a placement can be a bridge from previous employment into a better or more congenial job. For all students, a placement allows you to use your new skills in a practical situation, and, most importantly, it gives you the chance to make contacts.

Getting a placement is often frustrating and time-consuming, but it is a real opportunity which you would be wise to take seriously. Every year many students get job offers as a direct result of their placement – either with the organization where they worked, or because the placement gave their CV just the required boost.

> Gwen, a mature student, did a placement with the company where she already had a part-time administrative job. She negotiated it carefully, realizing that she ran the risk of just being used in her existing job without learning anything new. However, the company took her seriously, introduced her to different parts of the organization and gave her a taste of more responsible positions. She seized her chance and made such an impression that she was invited to apply for a more senior position after she graduated – she was also promoted in her part-time job! The key to this success was her careful and detailed negotiation about what she hoped to learn and her enthusiasm when she was doing the placement.

Here are some of the opportunities a placement may provide:

- Skills or techniques you have learned in the classroom may be put into practice.
- Theoretical understanding can be observed and tested in real life.
- Relevant experience to put on your CV.
- You can find out how you might strengthen your CV even more – what experience or qualifications do employers look for?
- It will boost your university reference by having an employer's view of your abilities.
- A chance to test out a prospective job.
- It will build your confidence.
- It's a great chance to do some 'information interviewing'.

Placements can be with all sizes of organization, from large corporations to one-man-bands, but it is always helpful to develop an awareness of what the organization is about. This will help you in choosing a type of organization you would enjoy working for (including working for yourself).

It's a good idea to negotiate a learning agreement with the organization before you start the placement – this means that both parties are clear about what is expected. Above all, go in with the attitude, 'What can I contribute?' The more you can give, the more you will learn.

Researching other options

Postgraduate study

If you're considering postgraduate study, it would be worth investigating your options just as thoroughly as you would a potential job. Of course graduates go on to higher study because they wish to pursue a line of research, or because they love their subject, but often they consider it because they haven't any other ideas, or because they assume a postgraduate degree would give them an edge in the job market. This is not always the case. If you're going to spend a year or more, and a considerable sum of money to do it, it's sensible to investigate just what you might gain.

Universities these days are in a market – they have course places to fill, and if the course is not very competitive they may take anyone who has the minimum qualifications and can pay. If a course seems vocational, for example, what jobs do its graduates go into? Can you find a past graduate who might tell you what to expect? What do people in the relevant industry think about the course?

Even if you don't expect the course to be vocational, you will also need to research sources of funding – and a few institutions offer their own bursaries, which might be worth remembering when choosing which university to apply to.

Full information on postgraduate study, including funding, will be available from your careers service. Look for postgraduate supplements and brochures and on the Prospects website (www.prospects.ac.uk).

Self-employment

There is now a lot of information available for new graduates thinking of starting their own business, covering everything from the personal qualities needed, to marketing, finance and tax. A good starting point would be the AGCAS booklet, *Self-Employment*, available from your careers service, or websites such as that of the National Council for Graduate Entrepreneurship (www.ncge.org.uk) which offers information and advice.

Self-employment needs just as much, if not more, research than any other career option and it is usually worth talking to people who have taken this route. The AGCAS booklet mentioned above lists many useful websites from arts councils, to Business Link. (See also later in this chapter, 'How do people find jobs?', pp. 71–77.)

Taking a year out

This is one option where research is crucial. Many more undergraduates fantasize about taking a 'year out' after graduation than actually do it, probably because they don't research the options. Do you mean a year? Where do you want to go? What do you want to do? (Gain work experience / travel / work to pay for a few months' travel / work as you're travelling?) Your careers service will have a lot of information on the 'year out', including books such as Susan Griffith's (2005) *Work Your Way Around the World*, and Margaret Flynn's (2002) *Taking a Year Off*. The more you start to find out what actually would be involved and what decisions you need to make, the more realizable your dream will become. (See also Chapter 6, 'Achieving your ambitions', pp. 145–148.)

How do people find jobs?

I once did a class exercise when we brainstormed how people find jobs using students' own experiences and that of their families. We filled a couple of flipcharts with how people had found jobs, such as:

- Saw an ad in the newspaper/journal/website
- Continuation of a placement
- I sent my CV to them
- Someone at a party invited my mum to apply for this new job
- I heard a friend was leaving and thought they'd want to replace him
- I was temping and they asked me to stay on
- Got it through an agency
- Applied on the Milk Round (employers' campus visits)

In other words, there are very many ways in which people find jobs. It follows then that there are many strategies for job-hunting. Let's look at some of them. (Note: For large organizations, and some professional postgraduate courses e.g. Postgraduate Certificate in Education, you need to be applying early in your final year.)

Finding vacancies in newspapers and journals

There are many places vacancies might be advertised, such as:

- *National newspapers.* 'Broadsheet' newspapers will have job sections, usually featuring different types of work on different days, e.g. on Wednesdays the *Guardian* advertises public sector jobs and *The Times* and the *Independent* feature business and finance opportunities. (Your careers service will give you full information.)
- *Local newspapers.* (Probably more useful for positions in smaller organizations, although big companies may sometimes use local papers to recruit staff who won't have to commute or relocate.) University careers services will have information on newspapers local to them.
- *Graduate vacancy lists.* Available from your university careers service or on-line, e.g. www.prospects.ac.uk Do remember when requesting these, that there are different types of graduate vacancy lists: those offering jobs that are available immediately, and those issued to final year students advertising jobs after graduation. The Prospects website is useful for identifying employers offering different types of work.

- *Professional journals* (or websites) related to different types of work are often produced by professional associations for a particular type of work, e.g. CILIP (Libraries) and Institute of Chartered Accountants have vacancy information. Local government positions are advertised on the web (see Further Information at the end of this book). Some of these journals may be available in larger libraries.

Sometimes you might come across a vacancy which interests you that's in a field you've never considered. Browse! If you're unsure about the level of job offered – whether it would be appropriate for a new graduate – you might want to ring or email the organization to ask.

Directories of graduate opportunities

Two directories listing graduate opportunities are *Prospects* and *Hobsons*. These substantial tomes are available free from university careers services. They are intended for final year students as they are advertising jobs available from the following summer. Employers pay a lot of money to advertise in these directories, so they usually feature employers who regularly recruit fairly large numbers of graduates (and who can predict their vacancies well in advance). Advertisers tend to be big industrial companies, retailers, banks, etc. They are certainly worth looking at as they contain a range of jobs from engineering to marketing, financial management to translation. For many students these directories are invaluable as they usually have a jobs index linking employers to types of jobs on offer. If, say, you are looking for a job in management consultancy, you can easily find a list of employers in this area. There are also directories which concentrate on particular occupational sectors such as retailing, banking, etc.

However, do remember that directories don't, by any means, show all graduate opportunities: it's estimated that only about 20 percent of graduates are employed by large organizations.

Employers campus recruitment visits (the 'Milk Round')

Some employers tour the country during the autumn and spring terms interviewing students on campus. Again, this tends to be larger employers with regular, predictable graduate recruitment. It's cheaper for them to send interviewers out than to pay interview expenses for hundreds of applicants. Not all employers visit all campuses – most will concentrate on larger institutions or those which offer degrees relevant to their recruitment needs. If your university careers service runs a Milk Round then this is an excellent resource to use as it gives you an improved chance of a preliminary interview. Most Milk Round organizations will also accept applicants from other institutions – possibly by advertising in general graduate vacancy lists. (A note here: some employers do restrict their advertising to specific universities.) However, it's important to remember that these companies are only a tiny minority of graduate employers.

Recruitment fairs

These are events where employers can meet graduates or final year students, and are held at different times at various locations around the country. Some are organized by university careers services, others by commercial organizations. Generally, they feature larger Milk Round-type organizations, but employers will vary. (There are some fairs dedicated to specific sectors, e.g. law, finance, public service, alternative careers). They will usually be advertised through the press, the Prospects website and careers services. Try to find information on who will be attending before you go, so you have an idea of whether they will be offering the sorts of jobs you're looking for. If they are, research the employer and go armed with a CV (see Chapter 5, 'CVs and covering letters', pp. 99–111), dressed and prepared as if you were going for an interview.

Agencies

There are all types and sizes of agencies, from those specializing in certain job areas (e.g. secretarial, financial) to general agencies. *Employment agencies* tend to find staff for temporary jobs; *Recruitment agencies/ consultants* often concentrate on more senior or specialized staff. Agencies make their money by charging the employer a fee for finding staff. Note that agencies are not allowed to charge you (unless they offer a separate service, such as help with CVs – but you can usually get this free from your university careers service).

There are many agencies on the Internet, some offering to circulate your CV widely. Remember however, that agencies aren't there to find you an ideal job – they exist to fill vacancies for employers. With new graduates they might find it difficult to 'pigeonhole' you – and might just concentrate on any jobs you have done in the past. They are an intermediary between employer and applicant, but you still need to make a professional impression, so when dealing with agencies be focused, punctual and smart.

Job centres can sometimes be useful for graduate jobs. Look in job-centreplus.gov.uk. The website has a job search facility by postal code – potentially useful if you're looking in one geographical area.

A foot in the door

If you had a vacancy would you want to spend money on an advertisement, have to deal with large numbers of application forms, spend hours arranging interviews and pay travelling expenses if there was an easier way of getting someone suitable? (To put it another way, if you were looking for a flatmate what would you do first: put an expensive ad in the local paper, put a notice in the students' union, or ask around among your friends?)

Employers know that advertising vacancies and interviewing is a poor way of finding a suitable candidate – it's much better if you already know someone who you think has potential and 'fits in'. This is why every year graduates find employment as a result of *work placements*, *voluntary work* or *temporary work*. Sometimes, with very competitive or glamorous jobs, a common 'way in' is through a lower level job. You enter the business, learn the ropes and keep your eyes open for opportunities to move up. Don't ignore this route: voluntary or temporary work can give you valuable experience and a chance to make an impression.

Applying speculatively: 'creative job-hunting'

Some jobs are never advertised because employers receive so many speculative applications they have a pool of CVs to choose from. Publishing houses, the BBC, record companies and similar 'glamorous' employers will receive dozens of CVs from hopeful graduates every year – and most of these applications will be extremely poor: some will not even be focused on a particular job (how can they guess what you're interested in, whether it's in production, engineering, accountancy – or cleaning?)

Properly done, however, speculative applications can be a very effective way of getting work. People do get jobs this way – not just with glamorous organizations but with others too. In fact, if you are limited to a particular geographical area, are career changing, or are looking at small- and medium-sized employers, creative job-hunting is one of the best techniques to use.

> Emily said she was looking for a job in publishing – but would be getting married and living in the Yorkshire Dales. I thought her ambition was impossible – but she got herself a job! Through very thorough research she found small local publishers; she then sent out a highly focused CV setting out just how she could help their business.

However, you cannot just send out a standard CV and expect it to get you an interview. Creative job hunting demands intelligence and persistence. If you are applying speculatively you must research the job and the organization so *thoroughly* that you can convince them that you can offer *just* what they need.

- *Research the job* and you will know exactly what it entails and how to target your CV, emphasizing your relevant experience and what you have to offer. Information interviews (covered earlier in this chapter) are especially useful tools in getting up-to-the-minute information about jobs and organizations.
- *Research the employer and their business.* You will need to make a good case for why you are contacting them, and how you may be able to help them perform even better. This means knowing as much as you can about their business, and finding out whom in the organization you should contact. (Don't send speculative applications to the Human Resources department – they are facilitators. You need to contact a front-line manager who knows that 'We need someone to do X . . .') Address your covering letter to that person.

> Helena was finishing a postgraduate course in interpreting and translating. She wanted to live in Germany, so she researched small- and medium-sized German companies who traded with the UK. She travelled over to Hamburg armed with her CV and went, literally, door to door to companies showing how her skills might be useful to them. None could offer her a full-time job, but several had work for her to do, so she set herself up as a freelance interpreter and translator.

Not only do people get jobs that aren't advertised – they also get jobs that didn't previously exist – by making such a compelling case for how their talents might be useful that they are taken on! This is an especially useful technique for mature graduates, career changers and people later in their careers, when they have a unique track record of experience.

After graduation Sean trained as a chartered surveyor. His ambition was to work overseas; to see some of the world. After investigation he thought that the insurance industry was a good bet and realized that loss-adjusting firms might value his surveying skills. He researched loss-adjusting, and some of the top firms, and then compiled a very carefully thought out CV selling his enthusiasm and expertise. He was invited to a couple of firms and received a job offer. After training in London he has worked in the Middle East, North and South America and the Caribbean.

What Color Is Your Parachute by Richard Nelson Bolles (2006) is an excellent job-hunting manual with a lot of useful information on creative job-hunting.

Networking

One of the best ways of finding jobs has always been through 'net-working' – or making contacts. When you're established in a job you'll probably do this automatically – you will meet people in similar jobs or similar organizations, and it's likely you will hear about opportunities arising. But what if you're just starting out, or you're changing occupations? How do you make contacts then?

Don't be shy about telling people that you're job-hunting and what you are interested in. You might gain contacts or ideas about jobs that you had never thought of. Do use information interviewing as a way of making contacts and introducing yourself to people.

Jason, wanting to work in the creative arts, interviewed the director of a small dance company: '*What advice would you give to someone like me, about to leave university?*' he asked the director. The answer he received was:

'Get as much experience as you can, voluntary or paid. Get to know people locally and make contacts. It's good to have a knowledge of where the funding comes from. Look at the Arts Council website and see what their 'vision' is for the next couple of years, and look at the community theatre and practice part. Look at the [local] council website. Make links with charities and other groups that do work within the community. You should read the industry magazines, *Big Issue, Young People Today . . .*'

Information interviewing can really pay dividends!

Self-employment

This is a growth area for graduates. There are opportunities for self-employment in many fields: painters, sculptors, photographers and other artists have traditionally been self-employed, but these days there are opportunities for all types of graduates. Many organizations and businesses now 'contract out' tasks which would once have been done by employees, and this means that there are now many more opportunities for people offering a wide range of goods and services – from health care to training courses, web design to catering. Sometimes it helps to have established a track record in an industry – a copywriter, for example, might gain expertise and contacts in the advertising industry before going freelance.

You need to give careful thought to what you hope to do, what resources and financing you would need, and what market you would be operating in. Research your business idea just as you would a job. Try information interviewing people, including potential clients; this is a good way to start making contacts. Careers services these days have a lot of information on self-employment, including details of local seminars and support networks such as the website www.businesslink.org (see 'Researching other options', p. 70).

Summary

- Thoroughly researching an occupation can help you decide if it's what you want and how to get into it.
- Reasearch may also give you other ideas.
- Thorough research will certainly help you write a better application form or CV.
- Use a variety of job-hunting strategies.
- Don't dismiss your dreams, investigate them!

5

Presenting yourself effectively

Recruitment and selection • Presenting your evidence • Application forms • CVs and covering letters • Interviews • Second interviews/ selection centres • Summary

Recruitment and selection

Imagine that you are a recruitment officer in a medium-sized organization. One day a manager from the marketing department comes to see you: one of her staff is leaving and they are looking for a replacement. What would you do? (Think about this for a few moments.)

What options did you come up with? There are several: first, you might ask if there's anyone suitable already working in the department, that is, you could *promote* someone into the job. If not, you might advertise it *within the organization* to give first bite of the cherry to people who are already on staff. (This is called advertising 'internally' – if you ever see a vacancy marked 'internal' it is open only to people who already work for the organization.) Then you might ask if there is anyone who is working in a temporary capacity in the department who shows promise. It's much cheaper and usually more effective to hire someone you know, who has demonstrated their potential to do the job, and who you know will 'fit in' with the other staff. (Hence the potential value of doing voluntary or temporary work.) Or there might be someone who has approached you about a possible job (see creative job-hunting in Chapter 4, pp. 74–76). If you are looking to fill a very senior post or you're looking for someone with very specific experience, you might make informal representations to a suitable person or engage a firm of 'head hunters' to make the approach for you.

If all else fails, you could advertise the post – which is expensive (paying for the ads), time consuming (doing a paper selection, organizing interviews) and, in practice, not totally reliable (how much can you tell about someone's competence from one interview?).

James wanted to work in housing management in a big university town where there was intense competition for posts. He couldn't move because he had a wife and children settled there. Instead of being unemployed, he got a job as a dustman. When a housing job came up, it was first advertised internally; being an existing Council employee he got a guaranteed interview – and he could demonstrate intimate knowledge of every estate in town! He got the job.

Job specifications and competencies

Whatever route they follow, the employer will almost certainly put together a job description or specification. This will describe the job and define what it requires, for example:

- qualifications
- experience
- any special aptitudes, e.g. numeracy, IT skills
- temperament required, e.g. outgoing, self-motivated, calm, able to make decisions
- any special circumstances, e.g. must be prepared to move house frequently, or to travel daily, or to start as soon as possible
- salary range offered

These days it's increasingly likely that the job specification will be based on the identification of key *competencies* required by the job. These might be things like:

- able to work in a team
- good intellectual ability
- able to set and achieve goals
- good communication
- willingness to learn
- able to manage their time
- creative
- persuasive
- able to fit in with others
- a risk-taker
- honest
- flexible/adaptable
- leadership
- hard working
- emotionally resilient
- self-reliant
- able to handle responsibility
- conscientious
- has common sense
- self-confident
- good at forward thinking
- empathetic
- good at planning and organizing
- has specialist knowledge
- good problem-solving skills

Obviously different jobs will require a different mix of competencies (including competencies not mentioned here). Think, for example, about what a policeman or -woman would need, compared with someone running a day care centre for the elderly. There will be areas of similarity but also great differences. Similarly, competencies will be developed differently according to what you have studied: problem-solving, for example, would be different for a philosopher than for an engineer.

It is really worth thinking about competencies as they're increasingly used, not only in recruitment but also in staff appraisal and training. Competencies are useful for you as a job applicant, because *they clearly signal what areas you need to focus on when presenting the evidence that you can do the job.*

The recruitment process

Let's look at what might happen if a job is to be advertised. A vacancy advertisement will be written. The problem here is that space costs money and so you need to keep it short. For this reason most vacancies ask applicants to send for more details, and possibly an application form, or they will give a website address.

Attention also has to be given to where to advertise the post: in a specialist journal? National newspaper? Local press? This will depend upon the type and level of the job. If the qualifications and experience required are highly specific, then the job might be advertised in the specialist press.

The vacancy will have specified a closing date for applications (usually applications arriving after this date will not be considered) and how to apply (e.g. by completing an application form, which enables candidates to be easily compared, *or* by sending a CV – hardly ever both). Sometimes, if the post attracts a lot of applicants, initial selection might be done by somebody relatively junior, or even by computer. (Some organizations, for example, do a preliminary sift by A level points: hard, but true.) Then all the selected application forms will be assessed *in the light of the job requirements*.

From those paper applications, relatively few will be selected for interview. This is because interviews are costly: they take staff time, and may involve paying travel expenses. It is vital, therefore, to write the best application you can or you have lost any chance of getting the job.

For many employers the first interview will be the only interview – an appointment will be made on the basis of this one contact. The interview may be one-to-one (one interviewer, one candidate) or it may involve a panel of interviewers. There may even be a series of interviews and exercises where all candidates work together (see 'Interviews' later in this chapter).

Some employers, especially bigger organizations, may use first interviews as another preselection stage. From a series of interviews (e.g. campus visits) they will choose a few people for a second interview. Second interviews are lengthy and testing procedures where short-listed candidates will undertake a series of interviews and exercises over one or two days. (There is even the odd employer, e.g. for fast-track civil service posts, which require a third interview!)

At each selection stage the people chosen to go forward will be those who most clearly *match the job specifications*. The recruiter will be looking for *evidence* that you have these competencies. Your task, as a candidate, is to provide it.

Presenting your evidence

The most important thing to remember is this: when employers are reading your CV or application form or interviewing you in person, they are assessing you, not on whether you are a likeable or fascinating human being, but solely *in relation to the job*. Whatever the questions, all application forms, CVs and interviews are really asking you:

- *What do you know about this job?*
- *What* evidence *can you give to show you can do it?*

When I was acting as a graduate recruiter it was always drummed into me that *the best predictor of future performance is past performance*. So the employer is looking for *hard evidence* that you have the skills and qualities or competencies to enable you to do the job well – or at least that you have the potential to develop them.

It follows that when you are writing your application you are aiming to *give evidence* that you can meet the requirements of the job. So the first step to making effective applications is to use your graduate skills to find out what those requirements are. In other words, to *analyse the job you are applying for.* Here's where your detailed investigations in Chapter 4, 'Researching occupations' (pp. 59–62), can pay off. You may be replying to an advertisement of a vacancy, in which case the requirements might be specified in a recruitment booklet, in the job advertisement itself or in further information which the employer will send you.

> I must admit that [researching] being a curator has made the task of writing a CV and application form that much easier. I now know what I should include, what I should leave out and what I should stress.
>
> (Tom, third year undergraduate)

Reading a job advertisement

If you are replying to a job ad, you might ask yourself:

- Who is the employer? (The ad may be from an agency.)
- Where will I work? (Not necessarily the same place as the head office address.)
- What are the hours?

- What's the salary?
- What qualifications are asked for (essential or desirable)?
- What experience is required (essential or desirable)?
- What is the ethos of the organization? (Will I fit in? Does it match my values?)
- How do I apply? (If it says 'apply in writing' send a CV and covering letter.)
- What's the closing date? (Don't wait until the last minute!)
- Note down the job title and reference number (if any).

And the most important question:

- What does the job involve and what skills, personal qualities or competencies are they looking for?

Ads in the Press are expensive so they are usually short; many employers will invite you to send for further details (or to go to a website) – which usually means a job specification – please *do get these details*!
Your task is to:

- analyse the job specification; and
- give *evidence* that you have (or can gain) these competencies.

This is what an employer told me recently:

'We had a vacancy and advertised it through the local universities. Although it was a 'starter' job I thought a lot of graduates would be interested, especially as our business is connected to film and TV. We did get dozens of applications – but almost all were unbelievably poor. I wouldn't have thought these people were graduates! They couldn't spell, wrote sentences without verbs and, most of all, really had no idea what an application form was for. We sent each applicant a detailed job description which had lots of clues to what we were looking for – and most ignored it. Instead of giving evidence about how they could do the job, they told us what they wanted! We offered the job to a non-graduate in the end.'

Researching the employer

As well as investigating the job, it's worth researching the employer. Your careers service will have information on large employers, such as their recruitment information and annual report. With small employers you may just have the vacancy to go on and often this gives very little information. In this case find out as much as you can about the employer using a web search or local libraries (business librarians can be invaluable at directing you to obscure sources of information).

It's important to understand the *business values of the organization* you're applying to. This is true whatever type of employer you're applying for, from a school to an international motor manufacturer – to find out if this is the sort of organization you want to work for and how to pitch your application. What sort of words are used in the ad or brochure? Examples could be: *fast moving, dynamic, tradition, family business, innovative, competitive, cutting edge, aggressive* – do these give you clues?

Employers often comment that graduates seem to have little understanding of the organization they're applying to, particularly in terms of what the organization's aims are and what markets they operate in. (This is not just true of large businesses – I once visited an artist who was looking to employ an assistant and she made exactly this comment.) You might find out:

- What does this organization do? (E.g., *manufactures chocolates; heals animals; promotes political change; protects the community; provides a service . . .*
- Do you know about the products or services it offers?

Examples of questions candidates have been asked:

- At an RAF selection board candidates were asked about the types of aircraft the RAF fly
- A theatre asked a candidate in detail about recent productions

---

- Why do they do what they do? (E.g., *to make a profit; to promote political change; to provide the best service possible within the allocated budget . . .*)

A publisher once told me that many excellent candidates applied for editorial jobs, but relatively few had commercial sense (i.e., realized that publishing was a business and books were marketed to make a profit).

- Who owns it? (*shareholders; trustees; family members . . .*)
- How is it organized? (*What is the management structure? Is it part of a larger organization, or bigger group of companies?*)
- What market do they operate in? Almost all organizations operate in 'markets' of some sort (E.g., a school will have a catchment area, a ceramic artist might be competing with others in his/her field or in the art market generally). Is their market local, national or international?
- What new technologies, legislation or developments might affect the way they do things? (E.g., global warming might boost the market for solar power; government initiatives might affect the Probation Service . . .)

To use a fairly simple example, take a local fish and chip shop. This will operate in a political, economic, legal, technological and social environment:

- political (may be affected by declining fish stocks)
- economic (the local factory closes, cutting demand)
- legal (health and safety legislation)
- technological (new equipment might mean a need for training staff)
- social (more people are eating fast food – time to expand what's on offer; people may now like to sit outside café-style)

If even a small fish and chip shop can be affected by so many considerations, think of the influences on a bigger business. These have to be managed.

In almost all cases you should be able to research information about the business or market the employer is involved in. *Employers do respond to applicants who have taken the trouble to research the job, the organization and the business environment it operates in.*

What do you see as the key issues facing the food retailing industry?
(Question on a graduate application form)

Is this job open to a new graduate?

The first 'proper' job after graduation is often the hardest job to get. This is because:

- you're likely to be competing with lots of other graduates with very similar experiences and qualifications, and
- it's hard to judge whether a vacancy is suitable for a new graduate or not.

It's easy to over-estimate your skills when they haven't been proven in a work context. Often new graduates apply for jobs which require more experience *in the workplace* than they can offer. Also, many employers comment that graduates have exaggerated ideas about the salaries they can command and therefore make inappropriate applications. However, all sorts of factors will operate: a friend of mine was employed after graduation in a job where he was told that he didn't meet the requirements but that they would take him on because they were desperate! (It was a very hard learning curve but he never looked back.)

The best thing you can do is to analyse the vacancy to see how many of the requirements you match. Very rarely will anyone meet perfectly all job requirements. Analyse which seem essential and which just desirable, and if you're in any doubt as to your suitability you could ring up to enquire if the job would be suitable for a newly qualified graduate. If in doubt, have a go!

Remember, that in most cases, being a 'graduate' isn't a magic passport to high level positions: be prepared to take a learning position and use your graduate intelligence and drive to take you further.

The new graduate's 'catch 22'

The first 'proper' job after graduation is often the hardest job to get. You can't demonstrate you have the right qualities because you haven't the experience, and you can't get the experience because you haven't been given a chance to do the job . . . What can you do about this?

- A work placement is an invaluable opportunity to get hard evidence of your suitability and skills on your CV and to make contacts (see Chapter 4, 'Making the most of a work placement', pp. 67–69). You may be able to negotiate a placement even if you have already graduated.
- Voluntary work could give you the same opportunities. It need not necessarily be in exactly the field you're looking for: you could demonstrate you have the necessary skills by, for example, working for a charity. (But it would, of course, be more advantageous to find voluntary work closely related to the job you hope to get.) In some very competitive fields, e.g. the media, people are often prepared to work for nothing in order to get a foot in the door. However, this is

open to abuse and you need to protect yourself from exploitation. Give yourself a time limit after which you will review your options, and keep your eyes open: what's happened to other people who have worked for nothing? Have any of them been taken on?

- Your job investigations (see Chapter 4) may have indicated that your chances will be boosted if you can gain an extra qualification. This may not need to be an academic award, it could be something you could learn in evening classes, or through distance learning, e.g. basic accounting, shorthand, IT skills.

Your personal inventory

Application forms and CVs require you to present *evidence* of your suitability for the job. This requires two strategies:

- Collecting the evidence
- Sorting and presenting the evidence as effectively as possible

In my experience, many graduates are very poor at presenting what they have to offer. Every year vacancies go unfilled because the right candidates couldn't be found – or perhaps the right candidates were out there, but didn't 'sell' themselves well enough to get an interview. One problem is that applicants don't offer enough evidence of their suitability. Most of us forget things we've done, or under-estimate their potential usefulness. This first exercise is aimed at collecting as much evidence as possible.

Your achievements

 EXERCISE 5.1

This exercise is to jog your memory and provide useful documentation when making applications or preparing for interviews. Time spent doing this as thoroughly as possible will save you a lot of time later. If you have compiled a graduate profile during your studies it should prove invaluable for this exercise. It may also be worth reminding yourself of your responses to the skills exercises in Chapter 3, 'Your skills', pp. 29–38. Note down as much as you can; you can sort out and select from it later.

1 Secondary education:
   List the following (please be accurate and give correct titles):

   • Schools/colleges you have attended from secondary level onwards
   • GCSEs or equivalents taken with dates and grades
   • A levels, Highers or equivalents with dates and grades

2 Higher education:

   • University or college, full title and address
   • Title of degree and dates of studies
   • What modules/courses have you studied? List them (with grades
     if possible). What did you learn in these modules? (Think not just
     of knowledge but also of other learning, e.g. working in groups;
     using spreadsheets; writing a report; devising an experiment;
     using statistics; etc. See your notes in Chapter 3)
   • List any other studies (e.g. extra courses, extra-curricular
     courses, professional qualifications, overseas exchange etc.) or
     training associated with a job (e.g. basic hygiene certificate,
     typing qualification, etc.)

3 Work history:

   • List all the jobs you have had, with dates. Note what organization
     you worked for (even if it was a small shop) and what they did, if
     it's not obvious (e.g. July–September 2005: waitress at Smith's
     Tea Rooms; December 2005: shelf stacker at Marlborough's
     Office Supplies Warehouse). Write down if the job was part-time
     e.g. if you did it alongside your studies.
        Don't discount jobs just because you think they were
     unimportant or low-level; even the lowliest job tells a prospective
     employer something about you. Some mature students may have
     had many short-term jobs; when it comes to a form or CV you may
     want to summarize them, but at this stage it's useful to list them
     as then you will notice any which seem, however remotely,
     relevant.
   • Note any voluntary work you have done. (e.g. scout leader; PTA
     treasurer; etc.)

4 Other achievements

- List any other qualifications you have gained or achievements you are proud of (e.g. Duke of Edinburgh's Award, Queen's Guide, diving certificate, coaching diploma, music exams, driving licence . . .)
- Can you speak or write any languages – to what level?
- List your computer skills (e.g. word-processing, using databases, web design)
- Write down any other skills or qualifications you can think of

5 Hobbies/interests:

- List your main hobbies or interests. Try to be precise: if you enjoy travelling, where have you travelled to? If 'football', do you play or just watch? If music, do you play or listen (e.g. grade 5 flute – play with the Springhill Wind Band)?
- If you have had any positions of responsibility (e.g. captain of Hall of Residence 5-a-side football team; secretary; treasurer; etc.) note them down.

REFLECTION 5.1

Have your hobbies tested you in any way or enlarged your horizons? How have you contributed?

6 What's missing?

Is there anything you have done which isn't included above and you want to add? (E.g.,I've owned a horse for 7 years and have a good knowledge and experience of stable management, and horse care. I have 'backed' a young horse and brought it up to basic dressage standard).

7 References

You will need at least two referees, one of whom is usually a university tutor. Ask at your institution what the system is for references (sometimes there is a centralized system so that you don't have to wait for a reference if your tutor is away). The other referee could be someone you have worked for or a friend. Always ask if you can use someone as a referee – never give their name without asking. This is not only courteous, it's sensible – if they are unwilling to give you a positive reference you need to know!

These exercises may have been time consuming but now you have a mass of information to draw upon when making applications. Students very often under-sell themselves on paper applications – they simply don't think to mention things they have done or to give concrete evidence of their achievements.

Choosing candidates for interview is often a question of mentally adding up pieces of evidence to present a picture of someone able to do the job. This evidence is cumulative – even small pieces of information (e.g. GCSE maths, a relevant degree module or a short-term job), could tip the balance. So give them the information: *if you don't write it down, they won't know about it.*

Summary

- Employers recruit to a job description.
- Your task is to compile and present the *best evidence* to show that you fit the job description.

Application forms

The application form is designed to help employers choose between candidates. They aren't choosing the nicest, brightest or most charming people; they are analysing applicants solely *in relation to the job*. The questions are there to elicit information from you *to compare with the job requirements*. The formal layout is to enable easy comparison between applicants (some large employers may use computer analysis to select candidates for interview).

It follows that your guiding rule when completing an application form is to *focus very closely on the requirements of the job* – which you have found out from the job description and from your research (see earlier in the Chapter, 'Presenting your evidence', p. 82). The form is your presentation of the *evidence* as to your suitability.

The biggest mistake students make is to regard an application form as something to 'fill in' as you would a driving licence application (i.e., give basic information without much thought). A good application will take time and careful consideration, but once you have done one you should be able to adapt the information for future use. It is just as much an intellectual exercise as writing an essay.

What do you think are the attributes that make you successful? How could you use these in your chosen career?

(Question on graduate application form)

One useful tip, before you start, is to write out the job requirements (taken from the job description) and to draft out opposite each requirement the evidence you can give to support your application. For example:

- *Self-motivated* – Duke of Edinburgh's Award, school prize, organized holiday hiking trip; found work placement . . .
- *Time management* – held down part-time job when studying, all assignments in on time, secretary of rowing club . . .

This will also be useful when you come to attend interviews.

Preliminary selection by phone

Occasionally you may be subjected to a mini-interview when just ringing up for an application form: this is clearly intended to weed out inappropriate applications at a very early stage. See 'Interviews' later in this chapter (pp. 111–125) and have your information and evidence ready, just in case.

Types of forms

Many employers will have their own employer application forms (EAFs). Large employers who regularly recruit graduates may have their own specific graduate application forms (available from your careers service or on-line). Some employers will use the Standard Application Form

(SAF) which was designed by some graduate employers and careers services together (these are also available from Careers Services and online). Only use a SAF if the employer has specifically asked for it.

You may also come across a form which asks to you answer multiple-choice questions and to tick boxes. These *'biodata' forms* are usually used by organizations which recruit large numbers of people into clearly defined jobs. They use psychologists to give a 'profile' of the characteristics of people already successfully doing the job and use these as selection criteria for future candidates. Selection is usually done by computer. The best advice is to answer the questions honestly. I'm told that they are actually more sophisticated than they look, but a little common sense, added to what you have found out during your research, may give you clues on what answers to avoid.

Completing the form

Your aim is to *present the strongest evidence possible in relation to the job requirements.*

Do read the form carefully and draft your replies before filling it in. Also, if you're writing the form, as opposed to typing it on screen, I would recommend that you use pencil first in your replies so you can make sure they fit the space available. Neat presentation is important: the employer has no obligation to read your form; if it's scruffy and illegible it will be discarded.

Let's have a look at some of the questions you might encounter.

Factual questions

These are the most straightforward ones: name, age, A levels and so on. But think about *how* you present this information. If you're giving a list of A levels or GCSEs make sure that the reader's attention is drawn to the most relevant ones and the most impressive grades. (Do also look at the form carefully: many students omitted their A levels/Highers on one version of the SAF because the design of the form was rather unclear.)

Academic qualifications

Many graduates put the briefest information on their forms (e.g. BA Hons French) However, if the job is related to your degree discipline, mention relevant courses, dissertations or special projects. Even if it isn't intimately connected, think of anything which could be relevant (e.g. a literature student who has done a module on children's literature could mention this when applying for a teaching course). Be aware that employers won't necessarily understand a module or even course title, so if your course isn't a common one, give brief details if you have the space.

Think creatively about your studies – a literature student applying for social work might not have any directly relevant modules but may have covered things like multicultural issues, which could be useful.

If you're going for a job that is not obviously related to your degree, the employer might not be too interested in what you studied (so the fact that your dissertation was on flood levels of the Upper Dee, or women in wartime munitions factories could be less relevant than the fact that you went out *interviewing* people to collect the data or that you used *statistical* techniques to analyse the data . . .). Don't forget that many of your college courses were probably designed specifically to give you skills that would be useful in future employment, so you could mention that you have engaged in field work, written reports, worked in groups, given presentations, etc.

What you write obviously depends on the space available and you do need to be concise. However, remember that a form is an *accumulation* of evidence, so you should be building up that evidence, piece by piece.

If you don't put your evidence on the form, no-one will know about it.

Employment history

Again, think about making the most relevant information stand out. If you have had experience in the field you're applying for, then this should be displayed to good advantage so that the reader notices it immediately. Even if you have no directly relevant experience, have you had a taste of the work environment you're applying for (e.g. do you know basic office procedures)? Or have you used relevant skills? For example, someone who has worked in a shop could, with imagination and intelligence, draw parallels with jobs in many areas: retailing, marketing, teaching (dealing with difficult customers at a busy time) . . . List all your jobs, as even the most lowly says something about you and your motivation. Voluntary work could be as useful as paid work in demonstrating what you can do, as could work placements.

A young female student always got interviews – employers were so intrigued by her holiday job working on the dustbins! She used it to demonstrate how she could 'fit in' with many diverse types of people.

If you have had many short-term jobs you may need to summarize them, emphasizing the most relevant. Try to show any progression (e.g. in responsibility) or any repeat employment with the same employer (which shows that you were valued). You might also want to mention any training you have had (e.g. short courses).

Value your life experiences: if you were a full-time parent, say so (you probably developed excellent skills in organization and time management). You may have developed team-working skills through voluntary work or the PTA. Skills are skills no matter where you developed them.

Follow the form's instructions precisely: the current SAF, for example, asks you to highlight the most relevant experience and 'note what you achieved'. You would be surprised how many students don't do this. What could an employer deduce from this – that the candidate can't be bothered, or that he/she can't be trusted to read documents carefully. . .?

Hobbies/interests/achievements

Remember that you are not just listing here that you enjoy music or macramé . . . you're giving *evidence* that you *fulfil the requirements of the job*. Give information in the order that makes the most impact. Don't hide significant achievements: if you've got a Duke of Edinburgh's Award, are a Queen's Scout, have attained Grade 8 in piano, are captain of the First XI, are a sports champion . . . let it stand out.

You may want to elaborate on your interests: being secretary of the Film Society, for example, could mean that you put up the odd poster or it could involve a lot of organization and administrative skills – if the latter is true, briefly give a flavour of what you do. Overseas travel, for example, could mean that you booked yourself a package tour or it could have involved a lot of initiative and self-reliance.

This section is often included to elicit clues about your personality: are you a mixer? Are all your hobbies quiet and solitary ones? Is your sole interest 'socialising' (whatever that means). Students often write 'social-ising' in this section – which could mean, 'I haven't got the energy or motivation to do anything useful with my time except party' or it could mean 'my friends are very important to me and I make sure I have time to spend with them'.) Do think about giving the right impression. If you have been working during your studies and have had very little time to do anything else, explain this: tell the employer just what your hours were.

Always think about:

* what you have gained from your hobbies and interests
* how this relates to the job,
* how you're presenting this on the page.

Difficult questions

Graduate level forms will probably be much more demanding than any you have done for vacation or low level jobs, and the most difficult sections will be the 'open ended' questions – here are a few examples from employers' application forms:

* *Describe a situation where you have overcome a set-back to your plans.*
* *Describe the most difficult decision you have had to make. Tell us how you reached this decision.*
* *What people, events and experiences in your life have you found difficult to handle? How have you coped and how have you developed as a result?*
* *What have been the most important events in your life so far? Indicate briefly why they are of significance to you.*

And how about this one (space left for the answer – one A4 page!):

* *Tell us about yourself.*

Questions like these are often the most important on the form: never, ever, leave them blank. They are inviting you to demonstrate your intellectual skills through the quality of the information you present, and how you organize and communicate your ideas. The responses will need careful drafting. Remember that you are giving *evidence* that you can do the job, so your answers should be related to the job requirements. Read the questions very carefully: they may explain exactly what is required:

> *Describe a challenging project, activity or event which you have planned and taken through to a conclusion. Include your objective, what you did, any changes you made to your plan and state how you measured your success.*

You would be surprised how many applicants don't follow these instructions!

Many graduates find these questions very challenging – but that is the point: they take time, thought, imagination and intelligence – and this in itself acts as a selection stage, to weed out those who can't be bothered.

One question that regularly turns up and which always seems to cause difficulties relates to *problem-solving* and will go something like this:

Describe a difficult problem you have solved, how you approached it and how you evaluated your actions.

'Problems' could be different in different contexts: how to travel overseas if you have little cash; how to set up an astronomy society; how to get rid of an unpopular flatmate; how to choose your dissertation subject; how to get a useful placement when your plans fell through at the last minute . . . The point about this question is to get information on your powers of:

- Analysis – what exactly is the problem?
- Creative thinking – what strategies could you use to solve it?
- Judgment – how did you decide what to do?
- Planning – what did you do and when?
- Evaluation – did you review your solution? What might you have done better?

Your reply should detail your actions. Common mistakes include giving very vague and general information in this section, where often more detailed and concrete evidence is required.

Try to give evidence from as wide a range of experiences as possible: for example, your dissertation might have been relevant to the job, but you shouldn't answer every question with evidence from the dissertation. This is true of the form as a whole – don't focus exclusively on one area of your life, however relevant to the job.

Other questions

The SAF gives you the opportunity to outline your *skills* (see Chapter 3, pp. 29–38, where you will have itemized many of your key skills).

If you are asked about your *career plans*, give evidence of your research into the job – don't be afraid of being specific (e.g. that you have talked to people doing the job). You could also explain why you are applying to this particular employer and show that you know something about the organization. Employers will react favourably to evidence that you have thoroughly researched the job and their organization – it shows commitment and drive.

Occasionally a form will ask if there is anything else you want to say. Use this space to your best advantage. If there is something you want to make clear but haven't had the opportunity, then use this space (e.g. why you changed courses after your first year). Look through your dossier of evidence of your suitability for the job: if there is evidence that you haven't been able to fit into the form elsewhere, use it here.

Some careers services offer sample on-line forms on their website. Many will offer feedback on your draft applications.

Your writing style in the form

Some graduates feel uncomfortable dealing with personal experiences on a form or they worry about sounding boastful. You can overcome this by concentrating on giving hard evidence and allowing the reader to make the inferences. It is more effective to give real and concrete descriptions of what you've done rather than go for grand claims presented in abstractions. Compare:

- *'During my degree I have developed my communication skills . . .'*

with:

- *'My degree has required me to give presentations to a class of 40, and to be able to argue a case in seminar discussion; I have written essays, a reflective journal and reports . . .'*

Anyone can make claims, but concrete examples are more convincing. 'I am very well-organized' is simply a claim whereas 'At the same time as doing my work placement I was researching and writing my dissertation and working three nights a week in the café' is hard evidence from which the reader can infer that you are hard working and a good time manager.

Use concrete nouns and simple, real descriptions to give a taste of what you've done. You will find that by using this approach your form will sound factual and businesslike, not egoistical. Use verbs that are positive (e.g. *'I organized, planned, negotiated . . .'*).

Compare:

- *'Two friends and I went on a camping trip to Scotland. I bought the food . . .'*

with

- 'Two friends and I planned a camping trip to Scotland. We negotiated different responsibilities: mine was to organize food and supplies . . .'

Which has more impact?

Language is especially important if you're applying to a large employer where the forms may be sifted by computer in the first instance. The computer may well be searching for powerful verbs reflecting important aspects of the job (e.g. *planned, organized, negotiated, managed* . . . etc.).

The form is your chance to present evidence that you can do the job: some will be strong (e.g. a relevant placement) and some will be weaker (e.g. a semi-relevant module). Your job is to accumulate as much evidence as possible and to organize your writing on the form so that the strongest evidence stands out.

Other tips

- Always draft the form if writing by hand, preferably on a photocopy, to get a sense of what space is available. Presentation is important.
- If you're asked to use black ink, use black ink, not blue (it might not copy well).
- The form should be neat and legible. A scruffy form gives the message 'I don't care about this'.
- Use a dictionary or spell checker. (e.g, driving licence, practice or practise?). Employers frequently comment on bad spelling.
- The amount of space left for a question is a guide to the length of your reply. If they leave you a page and you use five lines, you probably haven't answered the question properly. If you haven't enough space, try to summarize; if necessary (e.g. if you're a mature student with a lot of work experience) you may need to add a good quality white sheet to the form, noting in the appropriate section that there is a continuation sheet. However, do try to keep to the allotted space if at all possible.
- Sometimes you may need a covering letter giving the job title and reference and mentioning where you saw the vacancy. You may want to add when you're available for interview (be as flexible as possible; if their interviews are already arranged they're unlikely to rearrange them for one candidate).
- Keep a photocopy. You'll need it to prepare for the interview.

More information on writing good application forms, plus copies of many employer forms, will be available from your university careers service.

Summary

- An application form is a presentation of evidence related to a job description.
- Present as much evidence as possible and organize the form so that the strongest evidence stands out.
- If you don't write your evidence on the form no one will know about it.
- Give concrete information, don't make vague claims.
- Make the form look neat and well organized.

CVs and covering letters

What a CV is and when to use it

A curriculum vitae or CV is a brief outline of your career so far. It should be used if a job advertisement asks for application to be made 'by letter and CV' or 'in writing', and also for speculative applications (where no job has been advertised). A CV should always be accompanied by a covering letter (see 'The covering letter' later in this chapter, p. 109). The CV and letter, together, are 'marketing' you.

Curriculum vitae is Latin for 'course of life', but don't let that fool you. A CV should never be just a list of things you've done. Like the application form, it is a presentation of *evidence* that you can do a particular job, and should be focused on the job description. It follows that you should adapt your CV for every job that you're applying for: one of the commonest mistakes is for graduates to write one CV and send copies out like fliers. In fact, because you have limited space in a CV, it is even more important that you really target the specific requirements of the job.

A CV should ideally be one or, at most, two pages: the whole point of the CV is to give relevant information in a concise format. Every line should count. This means that you will have to make decisions about what information you include and how you present it on the page. Small details can make all the difference to the impact your CV makes.

You will have analysed the job you're applying for and drafted evidence to show you can do it. Just as with the application form, you now need to present as much evidence as possible in a way that *highlights your strongest selling points*. One of the most important decisions to make is what format of CV to use.

There are many different ways of writing CVs. In this book I'll cover a couple of usual formats, but please do investigate others, as different layouts may be more useful for you personally or for specific situations. Your university careers library will have dozens of sample CVs for you to look at.

What to put on your CV

Let's have a look at some of the areas you will cover in your CV (they needn't be in this order). (See also 'Application forms', earlier in this chapter, p. 90, for tips on presenting information.)

Personal information

- Your full name (it could head the page)
- Address, telephone number and email address
- You may want to include your term-time address if you're still studying

You might also include:

- Date of birth or age, sex or nationality
- Marital status, number of children and their ages
- A photograph

This may require some thought: you don't want to invite discrimination. However there are some jobs where it would be a positive advantage to, for example, have had experience bringing up children.

Education

Concentrate on your highest qualifications from secondary education onwards. Give the name of your school and university, dates attended and a list of exam passes, with grades if they support your application. You don't usually need the full address of your school, but the location can be useful (e.g. St Bede's Comprehensive, Leeds).

Think about the chronological order you're using. Remember, the aim is to make the maximum impact, so it usually pays to start with your most impressive qualifications – usually postgraduate or undergraduate studies, then progress to HNDs, A levels or Highers and then to GCSEs. Give the name of your university and name and location of school(s). Remember that you're not simply giving information – you're giving *evidence that you can do the job*, therefore, emphasize any relevant courses studied (see earlier in this chapter, 'Application forms', p. 90) – this might mean giving details of specific modules studied, or starting a list of A levels or GCSEs with the most relevant subject.

Many undergraduates fail to mention their degree course on the grounds that they haven't graduated yet. Or they just write, 'BA Hons. History' and no more. Please do think about giving fuller information on your degree; graduates applying for their first 'proper' job may not have had much relevant work experience and therefore need to make the most of anything relevant in their studies. Remember that a reader may not understand module titles – or even what your degree course, as a whole, involves – so you might have to give a short synopsis: if your French degree was business-orientated, for example, you might mention this. Remember – you're not listing information, you're *presenting evidence*.

Think creatively and positively to link your experience with the requirements of the job. IT skills, for example, are useful for almost anything these days, so you might want to mention any courses that covered IT. If you failed in something, you don't have to mention it. You could mention grades achieved if they were good, and any prizes or awards.

> Peter was applying for work in journalism but never mentioned (until prompted) that his degree course had developed skills in word-processing, desk-top publishing, and interviewing!

Include any short courses, on-the-job training or other qualifications achieved (e.g. through evening classes), either here or in a separate section on professional development. You might have had on-the-job training, for example, in first aid, safety or food hygiene, which might sometimes be useful to mention.

As your career progresses, lower qualifications will recede into history and your CV will probably be mainly taken up with work experience. Do make sure you keep a record of any training you are given, as you never know when it might be useful in future applications.

Employment

Give the dates of employment and the name of the employer (it's sometimes worth mentioning what they did, e.g. Bates and Co. (light engineering works); Smith and Briggs (shoe shop). You don't usually need to give their address. Give your job title and/or brief information on your duties. Always focus on anything relevant to the job you're applying for.

Some students omit jobs because they think they're too low level or unimpressive, but almost any job can say something about you, and your motivation – for example, that you found the job, and stuck with it. Voluntary work and work placements can be as useful as paid jobs. If you have had a large number of short-term jobs you may want to summarize them. (More information on presenting your employment history is given in 'Presenting your evidence' and 'Application forms', earlier in the chapter, pp. 82–99).

Remember, if you started the Education section with your degree, then you must *keep the same chronological order* in the employment section too (i.e., usually the most recent jobs first). If a previous job is more relevant then you may want to use a different order and you may want to start your CV with an Employment section.

Interests/leisure activities/achievements

This section can be included to give an idea of what sort of person you are – a more rounded picture of you as an individual. For example, being in a music band or a team could indicate you have the ability to work with others. Achievements such as the Duke of Edinburgh's Award demonstrate your motivation. Voluntary work would be especially useful if applying for charity or social work; travel could show your self-reliance, etc. Remember that the reader will be making inferences: *Are these all solitary pursuits, if so why? Is this someone who sets themselves goals and achieves them?* Always think about the impression you're giving: you would be surprised how many CVs simply list hobbies in any order: *supporting Arsenal, Chinese cooking, Duke of Edinburgh's Award (gold), DIY . . ..* Make impressive or relevant information stand out! (*Duke of Edinburgh's Gold Award; Chinese cooking; basic DIY; loyally supporting Arsenal; . . .*) Also think about giving brief details if it helps to better present your skills (e.g. treasurer of rowing club – controlling budgets, fund-raising, etc.).

Other information

There may be other things you want to include, such as non-academic qualifications, languages, music grades, first aid training (look in Chapter 3, 'Your interests', p. 43). Make sure you find a place to put these – if necessary use an Other Information section. If you don't mention achievements, the reader won't know about them.

You may also decide you would like to use a Personal Statement or Career Goal section, explaining why you want this type of job, or to work for this employer. Always use a CV format that best presents the evidence you need to give: for example, if you're writing a CV for an academic post you will emphasize research, publications, conference presentations, teaching experience, membership of professional associations, etc. There are many possible ways of writing a CV – it's worth exploring different formats and choosing the one which best suits your purposes.

Be careful about including information on political or religious affiliations (unless they're so much a part of your experience that they're unavoidable). You don't know who will be reading your CV and what their attitudes are, and you don't want to attract prejudice unnecessarily.

How to present the CV

Chronology

It really is important to consider what chronological order you are going to use: are you going to start with earlier events or put the most recent experiences first? I would suggest that you always use the order that makes your most impressive or most relevant achievements stand out. For most people that means starting with their degree studies, using reverse chronological order. *Whichever order you choose, keep to it throughout the CV, in all sections* – otherwise it is very confusing for the reader.

Layout

Presentation is very important. The whole point of a CV is to present information clearly and concisely: one glance should show the reader how it is organized so they can find information quickly. It's absolutely crucial to pay attention to headings, fonts, font sizes and 'white space' on the page. Even things like lining up columns of text will create a good or bad effect. If your CV runs to two pages, use the whole of each page – either allow more 'white space' or use a slightly bigger font.

If you don't have visual skills, get a friend who has design expertise or sensitivity to give you feedback. If necessary, use a standard CV word-processing template (but make sure that it gives you scope to present the information *you* need to present.) Use good quality paper and a good printer. Remember, when typing, that a comma is followed by one space, a full stop by two.

I would very strongly recommend that you show your draft CV to a careers adviser or someone who can give you authoritative feedback on how you're presenting yourself (they will need to know about the job you're applying for). It is absurdly easy to omit information, make spelling mistakes or use a confusing layout.

Some people like to include a photograph. It's not essential, but it could create a more personal and memorable impression. But please don't just send any old photo; make sure you look friendly but business-like, not as if you've crammed into a booth with your mates after partying all night!

Language

Some people prefer a CV written in a formal, impersonal register (voice), even to the extent of objectifying oneself: '*A determined, goal orientated person . . .*' (on a personal statement). Others like to use 'I'. It's a matter of choice, but bear in mind the type of organization you are applying to.

Think also about the language you use: do you use dynamic verbs, e.g. *managed, organized, researched, succeeded, coordinated* etc., or are you subtly underplaying what you did?

- '*To research my dissertation I went on a camping trip to the Atlas Mountains . . .*'
- '*To research my dissertation I organized a camping trip to the Atlas Mountains with three fellow students. We negotiated and delegated responsibilities; mine was to research and coordinate transport . . .*'

Write for impact and effect, and support your claims with concrete examples so it doesn't sound as if you're inflating your achievements.

Computer-sorted CVs

As with application forms, some large employers scan CVs into a computer and sort according to predetermined criteria. By picking out *key words*, e.g. *team-building, communication, managing money*, etc., they can sort thousands of CVs. If applying to a large organization you need to bear this in mind: think about the words they will be looking for, and focus your CV accordingly.

If you're applying on-line, check that your CV will be privacy protected.

Examples of CVs

Here are two sample CVs. The first, by Paula Harris, is fairly simple in design and is being written by a final year student looking for a job in nature conservation. Note how she's trying to foreground anything relevant, including possibly relevant modules in her degree even though she hasn't yet graduated.

The second, by Stephen Wilson, starts with a Personal Statement and lists skills relevant to the job. Stephen is slightly older than most students as he didn't do A levels but had a variety of short-term jobs. He's summarized this – giving some details as it could be useful for a journalist to have had an insight into different jobs. In his covering letter, I would expect Stephen to briefly explain that he left school after taking his GCSEs and why he subsequently went to university. (If I were interviewing him I would want to find out if he would settle into a permanent job.) In the Employment section Stephen starts with the bar work (the least relevant job) because he needs to keep a consistent chronology. He is, however, always looking to emphasize relevant information.

These CVs are only examples – they aren't meant to be outstanding. Many more examples – including some giving different formats and layouts – will be available from your careers service. If, for example, you're applying for a job where design or creativity is important, you may want to do a more creative CV – using visual imagery, or a more idiosyncratic layout. You may want to use colour, photographs or a more imaginative design. Choose a format which best enables you to present the evidence that you can do the job, and which seems to fit with the type of organization you're applying to.

CURRICULUM VITAE
PAULA HARRIS

Date of Birth 13th March 1984

Term Address	**Home Address**
13 Wells Street	4 Station Parade
Moortown	Sandy Beach
MZ12 3NQ	DR2 1BZ
paulaharris@email.net	Telephone: 0777 7777

Education

2003–06	**University of Moortown** BSc Hons **Environmental Sciences** (2:1 expected) Modules include: Conservation, Environmental Law, Marine Biology, Community Ecology, Hydrological Processes, Applied Chemistry. Final year dissertation on effects of coastal erosion on marine life.
1997–2003	Hewett School, Sandy Beach, Dorset
A levels	Biology(B), Chemistry(C), Geography(C)
GCSEs	10 including Maths, English, Physics

Employment

2004–present	**Masons Arms, Moortown** Waitress / bar work in busy pub. Evenings and weekends during term time.
November 2005	**Bond Green Conservation Trust** Work placement: coastal and woodland management on this newly established nature reserve. Practical and office duties including input into dunes regeneration plan.
Summer 2005	**Black Wood Nature Reserve, Bridgetown** Practical woodland management, fencing, paths, etc. Data collection for mammals survey. Designed worksheets for visiting schools.
Summer 2003	**Cheapo Supermarkets** Counter assistant and cashier. Often left in charge of the bakery on late night shifts and responsible for the reductions of products and customer enquiries. Enabled me to work in a team environment as well as independently and was a great opportunity to improve my communication skills.

Interests

- Duke of Edinburgh's Silver Award; First Aid Qualification; Outdoor Young Leader's Certificate.
- Founder member Moortown University Ecology Society, Treasurer 2005–06; organized ongoing help with upkeep of local 'wildlife' part of cemetery.
- Member of Woodland Trust, took part in plantings, fund-raising, etc.
- Badminton, running for fitness.
- Music: listening to live bands.

References

Ms S. Castle, Director	Dr Stephen Mole,
Bond Green Conservation Trust	Dept. Environmental Science
Bond Green	Moortown University
Moortown MZ20 3TZ	Moortown MZ2 2DJ

Curriculum Vitae
STEPHEN WILSON

Personal Statement
An ambitious, gregarious and highly motivated graduate looking for sound training in journalism.

Writing Skills

Work experience on *Moortown Echo*, including two published features.
Have sold two freelance articles including travel piece to *Smart* magazine.
Writer and sub-editor on student newspaper for two years.
English degree involved researching and writing essays.

Other Communication and Interpersonal Skills

Final year careers module involved learning to interview (open questions, body language, etc.)
Giving presentations was integral part of degree.
Bar work involved listening skills, being able to spot potential problems and defuse tension.
Team working in university assignments involved negotiating responsibilities and motivating others.
Mix well with all types of people through summer factory work.
Course representative (liaison between department and students).

IT Skills

Expertise in word-processing, desk-top publishing, PowerPoint, web searches – including using Apple Macs.
Familiar with spreadsheets, databases.

Self-motivated

Managed degree studies and part-time job during term.
Set up informal 5-a-side college football tournament and managed team.
Solo travel in Romania and Hungary.
Self-taught guitar.

Education

2003–06	**University of Moortown**
	BA Hons English Studies
	Modules included Creative Writing, Research Skills,
	Using IT, Contemporary Writers.
	Dissertation on The City in Contemporary Fiction.
2002–03	Coketown College
	Access to Higher Education course (evenings).
1995–2000	Fawn School, Coketown
GCSEs	5 including English

Employment

2003–date	Barman and occasional waiter, Red Lion, Moortown
	(part-time evenings and weekends).
May 2005	Work placement with *Moortown Echo*
	Going out with reporters, attending court, shadowing sub-editor, also researched and wrote published features on Moortown Festival and Harry Parker (local historian).
Summers 2004, 05, 06	Halibut Brothers Ltd, Coketown (packaging company).
	Production line – loading, quality checking, etc.
2001–3	Coketown Council, Planning Department.
	Clerk, dealing with planning applications.
2000–01	Series of short-term jobs including factory work, office temping with estate agent, solicitor, manufacturing company, insurance agent, etc.

Interests

Politics and current affairs; travel (have visited USA, Spain and organized solo trip to Romania and Hungary); 5-a-side football as player and team manager; music – listening to new bands, playing the guitar and drums.

Personal Information

Date of Birth: 11.9.83

Term Address	**Home Address**
1 June Road	4 Otto Street
Moortown	Coketown
MZ1 4BQ	CT18 5SS
bazzo@email.net	Telephone: 0777 1111

Referees

Ms Tomasina Paper	Dr Peter Ware
Moortown Echo	Department of English Studies
Moortown	Moortown University
MK2 3BB	Moortown MZ20 3TZ
tomasinapaper@moorecho.net	peterware@moortown.ac.uk

The covering letter

A CV should always be accompanied by a covering letter. This should usually be no more than a page long and its purpose is to make the employer want to read the CV.

If responding to a job advertisement, give the job title, reference number (if any) and say where you saw the ad. Then concentrate on what you have to offer, matching the job requirements with your experience and qualifications. If there is anything you feel you need to explain, e.g. a change of career direction, do so briefly.

Below is an example of Paula Harris's covering letter in response to a job ad. Notice how she's emphasizing relevant experience, and the fact that she's bothered to research the organization she's applying to.

If you're applying speculatively rather than to a job ad then your letter needs to be *highly focused* on what you have to offer. The reader needs to think you are the answer to their problems! This obviously involves a great deal of research. Emphasize how you can help the organization, briefly outlining what you have to offer (see Chapter 4, 'Creative Job-hunting', p. 74).

Make sure your letter is addressed to the right person (and their name is spelt correctly). A speculative application must be sent to the appropriate person and never just to Human Resources. Remember if addressed to a specific individual a formal letter ends with 'Yours sincerely', otherwise 'Yours faithfully'.

13 Wells Street
Moortown
MZ12 3NQ
paulaharris@email.net

Mrs M.E. Smith
Head Warden
Green Bay Nature Reserve
Pembrokeshire   13th June 2006

Dear Mrs Smith,

   I wish to apply for the post of Nature Warden (Ref: RE627) as advertised in
The Guardian on 12th June.

As you will see from the enclosed CV, I am about to graduate from the University
of Moortown with a degree in Environmental Sciences (2:1 expected). My course
has covered marine environments and my final year dissertation was on the
effects of coastal erosion on marine life in the inter-tidal zone.

I am keen to start a career in nature conservation and am particularly interested
in working within an environment as diverse as Green Bay (which I have visited
as well as researching it through your website). My final year work placement
was with Bond Green Conservation Trust, a new nature reserve which, like yours,
includes both coastal and woodland areas. I enjoyed every moment of this
placement, which gave me an insight into the challenges faced in managing a
protected environment.

Last summer I also worked for Black Wood Reserve, near my home. This was
equally enjoyable although very different as it is ancient woodland. In this job
I learned practical skills such as fencing, and maintaining paths and drainage,
as well as office skills such as reception and maintaining accurate records.

I am physically fit and very adaptable: I have an Outdoor Leader's Certificate
and First Aid qualifications. I do hope you will consider me for the job. I am
available for interview at any time.

Yours sincerely,

Paula Harris

Paula Harris

Summary

- A CV isn't just a life history, it is *evidence* that you can match the job requirements.
- Don't use a standard CV: tailor it to the job. Speculative applications must be particularly tightly focused on what you have to offer.
- Present all the evidence you can in a way that draws attention to the most relevant. Hard evidence is better than grand claims.
- Think carefully about chronology, layout and language.
- Try to get someone to check it.
- Always send a covering letter with a CV.

Interviews

If you're invited to interview, congratulate yourself; you've already overcome major hurdles. Now the interview is the final make or break selection stage. You need to make the right impression, and you will, if you prepare for it.

Before the interview

First, some simple logistics: look at the invitation and check the date, time and location of the interview. (The location might not be the same as the address on the letterhead.) Check that you can get there on time. (If you can't, ring the employer immediately – they may be prepared to pay overnight expenses, or to reschedule the interview for later in the day). Write back confirming that you will attend on the day and time shown.

The letter may also give you some idea of what to expect. For example, if the interview is to be held over a whole day (or more), you could expect to be involved in exercises with other candidates (see 'Second interviews' later in the chapter, p. 125). If they ask you to prepare something, e.g. a presentation, then do read very carefully what is required and spend time over it.

It's worth checking also that you have something appropriate to wear. A good rule of thumb is to wear what someone working there might wear, but a bit smarter. Shine your shoes, don't go mad with the jewellery or make-up, try to be well groomed, tidy and clean. Not all organizations are formal, but you need to give the impression that this interview is important to you. However, you might be involved in factory tours or be working hard on group exercises on a hot day – so try to choose something comfortable and adaptable. You don't want to be distracted by your sore heel, or a tight waistband.

> *I observed the dress code in the car park . . . and dressed to match.*
> *I even practised handshakes with my flat mates before I left . . .*
> (Sarah, final year history student)

Most interviews will either be one-to-one or involve a panel of selectors (see below).

What questions will they ask?

An interview is a structured exchange. The interviewer is trying to get information upon which to make judgements about your suitability for the job: not whether you're nice, bright or fascinating but whether you are the best candidate for the job. Interviewers have the responsibility for making this judgement and they don't want to get it wrong. Your task is to make it easy for them by having the evidence ready. Look back on the research you did on the occupation or on the job description. You have worked out what they are looking for (in terms of things like qualifications, experience, personality, skills or competencies) and you have already given enough evidence of your suitability for them to feel it is worthwhile calling you for interview. Now they will be testing this evidence. For example, if you said you learned team-building when working on a group project, the interviewer might probe that in some detail. What exactly were your responsibilities? How did you overcome any problems?

They might structure the interview according to *biographical information* (looking at your history):

- *'Why did you choose to study psychology?'*
- *'What exactly did the work placement involve?'*

or in terms of the *competencies* or requirements of the job description:

- *'Give me an example of when you have led a team.'*
- *'Describe something you have planned and organized successfully.'*

All interviewers know that *the best indicator of future performance is past performance.* This is why they will be looking for evidence of things you have done, situations you have dealt with, decisions you have taken, and problems you have overcome.

* *'Give me an example of a time you set yourself a goal and achieved it.'*
* *'Have you ever worked in a team where some people haven't been pulling their weight? What did you do?'*

Short anecdotes can be more memorable and convincing than pat replies.

Here's an example of a candidate explaining how she solved a problem in her voluntary job:

'When I was on duty at the animal shelter we had problems with one of the newer volunteers. She was well meaning but really unreliable and didn't always finish all her jobs. The rest of us wasted valuable time checking up after her – have all the animals been fed and cleaned out? It seemed easier just to do things ourselves. I didn't think this was right so I decided to speak to her. I was friendly but tried to be firm – I told her she was making life more difficult for the rest of us and, whilst we appreciated her help, if things weren't done properly in fact she was no help at all. She seemed surprised, and we agreed that she would do fewer kennels but would absolutely guarantee that they would all be finished. She did this, and we didn't have any more problems.'

If the job is related to your studies or previous experience they might ask *technical* questions to probe your level of knowledge.

Interviewers will be trying to find out:

* *Can you do the job?* Have you got the skills, knowledge, experience and personality? They will be interrogating your background in relation to the job description.
* *Will you do the job?* How motivated are you? Do you appear enthusiastic, well informed, well prepared and interested in the job and the organization? Are you someone who is used to achieving goals? To find this out they need to find out about your experience and your attitudes.

- *Will you fit in?* Are you the type of person who will work well with your colleagues and share the values of the organization?

Here are some fairly predictable questions:

- *'Why have you applied for this job?'*
- *'Why have you applied to this organization?'*
- *'Who else have you applied to?'*
  (i.e., is this a whim or a considered career plan?)
- *'Give me an example of a time when you showed leadership* [or another competence].'
- *'Tell me about yourself.'* (Focus on the job requirements rather than your life story – emphasize your goals, why you want the job and why you think you can do it.)
- *'What do you consider your strengths and weaknesses?'* (It's tempting, but unconvincing, to give mock weaknesses – e.g. 'I tend to be too conscientious' – self-awareness is a useful trait, try to be believable without damning yourself.)
- *'What do you consider your greatest achievement?'*

Remember that the interviewer is always looking for hard evidence that you can and will fulfil the requirements of the job.

Research the Job

You can expect to be probed about your motivation – why do you want the job? How much do you know about it? Here's where your research into the job will pay off – the fact that you have learned about the job and, if possible, talked to people doing it, indicates that you are really interested. (So make sure that you get across the fact that you have researched the job thoroughly.) If you have researched the job and analysed what you have to offer in relation to it, you have a powerful armoury of evidence ready to present at interview.

 EXERCISE 5.2

1 Look at the job description. List the requirements of the job in terms of skills, experience or competencies asked for. *If you were the interviewer*, how would you find out if the candidate (you) has these competencies? What would you think were this candidate's strengths

and weaknesses in relation to the job? What questions would you ask? What areas of your experience would you probe?

2 Now, looking at your form or CV, list the evidence you will give to demonstrate that you have these qualities. Use the strongest evidence you can, from all aspects of your life:

- What is the strongest evidence that you can do the job?
- What are the weak points – i.e., experience or skills that you lack?

Look at what you consider your strongest evidence, and *make sure that you will get this information across.* Go to the interview determined that, at some stage, you will mention your IT course, work experience, dissertation project or whatever it is.

3 Think about the weaknesses (few of us fit job requirements perfectly). How might you compensate for these? If there is something negative in your career history, like failing a course or leaving a job after a short time, be prepared to answer questions on it. Honesty is usually the best policy. Self- awareness and the ability to face up to unpleasant truths can show maturity. Try to think of positive things you gained from the experience. For example: *'I failed my first year exams and had to repeat the year. I'd spent my time enjoying student life without much thought about what I was doing. Failing was a real shock, and made me pull myself together. I realized I couldn't just wing it any more . . .'*

Research the employer

(See also 'Presenting your evidence' and 'Application forms' earlier in this chapter, pp. 82, 90.) Find out as much as you can about the employer. If applying to a big organization this will be easy – they might have a website or a file in the careers library which contains recruitment literature, annual reports, etc. For a smaller employer you may have to research in a local business library, or in the archives of the local paper. Find out what you can – the mere fact that you have tried indicates that you are keen to get the job. For example, if you're going for a retail job, they will expect you to have noted the layout of their shops, what types of goods they sell, seasonal trends, etc. They may ask you to offer suggestions about how you might increase sales.

Research the industry/sector

You can make a great impression if you have really researched the industry or sector this organization operates in. As I've said, one of the things employers most complain about is that graduates seem to lack business awareness. Some questions you might be asked are:

- *'What do you think is the biggest problem facing this sector today?'*
- *'What new markets might we move into?'*

Give yourself a head start by being knowledgeable: read the newspapers (search on-line for relevant articles), trade or professional journals. This applies whatever you're applying for, from nursing to production management. All organizations – from a ceramics artist to an oil company – operate within a business context. (See 'Researching the employer', earlier in the chapter, p. 83.) You may well be asked about why you applied for a job in this sector and what you think current issues are. For example: the fragmentation of TV viewing (the media); the introduction of the Literacy Hour (teaching).

An interview will never go exactly as you expect, but if you're on time, smartly dressed and well prepared, your confidence will be boosted before you even start.

During the interview

Assume you're being assessed *from the moment you walk on to the premises*. If you have to wait for your interview, your conduct with other candidates or staff you come into contact with may well be noted. Be polite and friendly at all times. If you have to wait, there may be house magazines or product brochures for you to look at – which will all give you some ideas about the organization. Remember that an interview is a two-way process: they are assessing you, but you also are deciding if you want to work here – so keep your eyes open. What are the working conditions like? What sort of place is it – very formal or relaxed? Would you like it?

First impressions are important. Consciously or not, interviewers assess the candidate as soon as they walk into the room; what they're wearing, how they move, whether they smile . . . So, be polite and friendly, shake the interviewer's hand (if invited), make eye contact, and smile. (Wet fish handshakes, wrestler's grip or averted eyes are very off-putting!)

Be open, friendly and, most important, show enthusiasm. Even if you're stomach is a nest of butterflies try to convey your enthusiasm for the job. It really does have an effect; you will come across as positive and energetic.

> *It takes a lot of energy talking about yourself in a positive way . . . It can be hard maintaining this for hours . . . I thought of it as like being on the radio . . .*
>
> (Sarah, final year undergraduate)

How might they structure their questions?

You will have prepared for possible questions, based on a comparison between your experience and the job description. (It's worth taking a copy of your form or CV with you.) We've already covered some of the questions you might be asked, so let's look at how they might be structured.

The interviewer can use different types of questions to elicit different kinds of information. (You could also make use of this section in preparing questions for your information interviews.) These are:

- *Factual questions.* Here your replies will give straightforward information: *What did your course cover? What were your duties as treasurer? What did the nursery job involve?*
- *Open questions* (which can't be answered by 'yes' or 'no'). These invite the interviewee to open up and often reveal attitudes, motivations, aspects of character: *Tell me why you chose to study zoology. What led you to apply for this job?*
- *Repetition.* If the interviewer repeats key words or phrases this is an encouragement for you to elaborate upon your answer:

  You: *I found the statistics courses really challenging*
  Int: *Challenging?*
  You: *Yes, I hadn't done stats before and realized I needed to catch up . . .*

- *Hypothetical questions.* These are 'what if' questions designed to test your ability to think on your feet, and your problem-solving strategies: *You've designed a marketing strategy based on TV adverts and in-store promotions. Two days before they're due to start, the TV channel goes on strike. What would you do?* Don't be afraid to pause to think about your answer – 'I need to think about this for a moment . . .' This shows confidence and a readiness to think before rushing to solutions.

- *Leading questions.* These offer you alternative answers: *'I see you changed course – was that because you couldn't cope or was the course not what you were led to expect?'* Beware of leading questions! Just occasionally they can be used to trap you. Remember that you don't have to agree with suggested interpretations. *'Neither. I was doing well, and it was a good course. I just hadn't realized that it was quite so focused on behavioural psychology, and I didn't think it would have helped me with my career plans.'*
- *Set questions.* Sometimes, particularly in the public sector, interviewers follow a strict and proscribed set of questions – asked in the same way and in the same order to all candidates. This way of questioning can seem very formal, even brusque or hostile. In fact, it's a way of ensuring that all candidates are treated in exactly the same way in order to ensure fairness. The questions will be very closely based on the requirements of the job, e.g. a list of competencies, and if you have prepared carefully you will be able to give your evidence clearly and succinctly.

Words to avoid

Never use 'just' or 'only' – these little weasel words will diminish your achievements: *I was only a housewife . . .* Change this to: *I was a full-time mother managing a household and two small children. . .*

Be careful about what you say and how you say it – almost all interviewers respond to a positive attitude and enthusiasm.

> *I once took on a woman on the strength of her having run a budgerigar club for six years. She did have relevant experience but had been out of the business for ten years. She was so enthusiastic about what she had done and the competitions and events she had organized . . . I really liked her enthusiasm . . . obviously she liked to be busy and had good organizational skills. She is now one of the most valued and efficient workers I have.*
>
> (Managing director)

Body language

As well as what you say, how you say it is important. We're told that non-verbal signals carry five times the weight of verbal ones, so it's definitely worth thinking about how you present yourself. Don't worry about feeling nervous – almost everyone finds interviews nerve-wracking, and the adrenaline can keep you on your toes. Interviewers won't usually mark you down for being nervous. (Don't, above all, disguise your nerves by being hostile or cocky – showing resentment will definitely make a bad impression.) However, adopting appropriate body language can help with the nerves.

Try this (practise it before you go):

- Sit facing the interviewer. If the interviewer is skilful you'll not be directly opposite them as this is rather confrontational; slightly sideways is more comfortable. Sit comfortably and *squarely* on the chair – don't squirm or loll or clutch the sides!
- *Don't hide* behind a bag or notepad – sit with your feet on the floor, arms open (not folded), or hands neatly on your lap.
- *Smile* and be friendly. Make *eye contact*.
- *Breathe deeply* and relax as much as possible. An interview is a two-way communication. You're evaluating the organization too.
- Before you go in, think of the most confident person you know. *Imagine* they dissolve into you – now enter the room as s/he would.

In class students practised being interviewed by a panel of their peers. Each interviewee was briefed to answer the questions honestly but *to adopt a particular body language* – such as superiority, hostility, inferiority, lying, etc. This is what a student wrote:

'I was pleasantly surprised by the last girl in our group. She hated this role-playing and said she hated job interviews and got tongue-tied at them. Ironically she was given the role of being self-confident, open and relaxed. She played the part full of confidence and looked in control of the situation. She seemed a different person . . .'

Interestingly too, the person giving 'liar' signals was seldom believed, even though they were briefed to tell the truth! Students are often surprised and impressed by this exercise: it shows that body language really does matter.

Practise being interviewed by a friend. They will notice if you're a foot-waggler or finger-tapper (things we can do when nervous without noticing). Or your careers service may offer mock interviews. Just as with anything else, your interview techniques will improve with practice.

Watch the interviewer's body language too. Their facial expressions and movements will give you *clues* as to when to expand your answers and when to stop. Usually interviewers are looking for candidates with good communication skills and that means being open and friendly, clear and concise. It's difficult to interview people who answer in monosyllables and also those who go on and on and on . . . If the interviewer allows a pause it's often an invitation to enlarge on your answer. If they interrupt you or summarize what you've said, it's a way of making you stop.

Try to make the interview easy for the interviewer: they are in control; they have the responsibility for gathering evidence and working within a tight time frame. Help them by being open, clear, concise, and having your evidence ready. Remember the interviewer is trying to find out if you will fit into the organization and will be looking for clues about your personality, sense of humour, social skills, etc.

Occasionally some interviewers use quick-fire questions, or they repeat the same question several times, to put the interviewee under pressure. This might happen if the organization is looking for someone who can cope with stress and confrontation. Even if the interviewer seems hostile, remain calm and patient and *never reflect hostility back*. They either are required to probe, or they might just be bad interviewers (they exist). Often, intensive questioning is a good sign – if you were a hopeless candidate, they wouldn't bother.

Questions you might ask

Usually you'll be invited to ask questions at the end of the interview. Don't ask a question just for the sake of it – it's annoying to be asked something which is in the brochure or job description. Similarly, questions about holidays, time off, etc. give the impression you're not a worker. At the same time, the interview is a chance for *you* to find out about the job, the organization and whether you would be happy there, so if something isn't clear, ask about it.

- *Where exactly might I be working?*
- *What happens next after you've finished interviewing? When might I hear the result?*
- *How are pay and performance assessed?*

Or you could subtly demonstrate your research:

- *Do you think the company will be moving into alternative technologies?*

If there's nothing you want to ask, say so.

• *No, I think the brochure and presentation have been very informative . . .*

Remember, the interview is also your chance to find out about the organization: is training given? Do they offer equal opportunities? Do people working here feel valued? What are the communication systems (e.g. are there regular meetings, briefings, etc.?) Some of these you might ask outright, others you might infer by what you learn during your visit. (See Further information at the end of the book for sources of information on organizational cultures.)

After the interview

Assume you're being assessed until you leave the premises. Afterwards, relax. You might think about what you did well, and what you might improve next time. (You will improve with practice.) Then let it go.

> *After the interview I thought I could have had better comebacks to some of the questions asked . . . I'm going to put it down to nerves . . . the building and the atmosphere were really daunting . . . I felt young and slightly exposed . . .*
>
> (Sarah)

Remember they were not assessing you as a person but *purely in relation to the job.*

Problems

Very occasionally, a candidate feels that s/he is being questioned inappropriately – for example asking a woman about her childcare responsibilities would breach sex discrimination legislation. If this happens to you, write down your memories of the questions immediately after the interview. You could then either take the problem up with the organization directly or tell your university careers service. The Association of Graduate Recruiters, Association of Graduate Careers Advisory Services and National Union of Students have agreed a best practice policy in relation to graduate recruitment. Copies are available from your careers service or on the Association of Graduate Careers Advisory Services' website (www.agcas.org.uk).

Different types of interviews

Panel interviews

These are when you are interviewed by a group of people rather than one-to-one. The panel may consist of the person who will be your line manager, your overall boss, someone from Human Resources, etc. A panel interview can seem intimidating but you should approach it just as you would an ordinary interview. The panel may take it in turns to ask questions, in which case you should concentrate on the person asking the question, but sweep your eyes over the rest of the panel from time to time. Don't be put off if a member of the panel seems detached or distracted – they might just be there as a formality.

All day interviews

One to one interviews are a notoriously poor way of finding the right candidate for a job, so some employers now use mini-selection boards. If you find that your interview is timetabled to take up a whole day you can assume that selection will involve more than just an interview – possibly there will be tests or group exercises. These types of interview are covered later in the chapter in 'Second interviews', p. 125.

PGCE interviews

These may often include some elements typical of second interviews (see later in this chapter, p. 125) such as group tasks, written tests (in maths or English, for example), discussions (e.g. on current issues in education), a critique of a video-taped lesson, a lesson plan or a presentation. Your research into the job and current issues will help you to prepare: do read the education sections of major newspapers and keep abreast of government initiatives (see Further information). There will be detailed information on PGCE interviews available from your careers service.

Telephone interviews

More employers are using this selection method as a cost-effective way of conducting preliminary interviews. They are unlikely to use it for their final selection, but it is a way of whittling down the potentially large number of candidates who appear promising on paper to get to the smaller number they will call for personal interview or selection board. Telephone interviews are usually preliminary interviews – so you have to get through them to go any further. They are particularly useful if telephone manner is an essential aspect of the job.

The employer might ask you to give a time when you can be contacted, or they may simply ring out of the blue and ask if you are free to talk immediately? If you aren't, then politely ask if you can arrange a more convenient time – even if it's only ten minutes later. Some of these interviews last up to half an hour and you need to be comfortable and prepared, with your papers ready and away from any interruptions or distractions.

Prepare for a telephone interview as thoroughly as you would a face-to-face interview: remember your focus should be on *putting across your strongest evidence that you can do the job*. Look at the advice on telephone interviewing in Chapter 4, 'Information interviews', p. 66 and make sure you are in a quiet place and have all the materials you need on the desk beside you – e.g. notebook and pen, and a copy of your CV or application form. Please don't eat or smoke – it's very off-putting for the person at the other end of the line.

Take trouble to be very clear in your replies: nuances of tone which are easily picked up in face-to-face interviews, when supported by body-language, simply aren't conveyed by phone. Think about the volume of your voice, its warmth and its vocal variety (think of monotonous lecturers and how their voices can drive you mad). It might help to stand up or move about. Imagine the interviewer is in front of you: this will help you to smile, for example, and will come across in your voice.

Students have said that it can be surprisingly off-putting when you don't get feedback from the interviewer. Make sure you listen extra carefully, as you won't be able to pick up non-verbal signals. If there's a pause, is the interviewer writing notes or waiting for you to continue? Are you talking too much and waffling or keeping on track? If in doubt ask, '*Would you like me to continue?*' You can, if necessary, ask for time to think, or for a question to be repeated, just as in a face-to-face interview (but it feels more awkward on the phone). Just try to be polite, business-like and enthusiastic.

Some employers are using automatic systems where, after applying for a job, you're asked to ring a freephone number and are then instructed to use the telephone keypad to choose between a series of statements about yourself or to answer a set of questions. These will be based on a personality questionnaire or aptitude test. They may well be timed as a way of trying to get authentic off-the-cuff responses. More information on these types of 'tests' can be found earlier in this chapter under 'Biodata forms' and later in the chapter under 'Second interviews' (pp. 92 and 125).

Video interviews

These are rare but some employers occasionally use them. Prepare as for 'ordinary' interviews, including taking care over your dress and appearance. Try to pretend the interviewer is in the room with you; listen carefully, be as relaxed as possible and try to convey your enthusiasm (this is harder if you're getting no human feedback). Address your replies to the camera rather than to a display screen.

Group interviews

These are where a group of people are interviewed together. Sometimes they are used as a way of preselecting candidates in person rather than via application forms. Listen to the questions carefully and try to judge whether you're required to work with your co-interviewees. A word of caution: brief group interviews are sometimes (but not inevitably) an indicator of questionable organizations. Remember that part of the interview process is for you yourself to assess the organization.

Interviews where you're known

These can be the most daunting. You may have been working as a temp and are going for a permanent job, or as an internal candidate looking to change jobs or go for promotion. It can feel strange to be formally interviewed by someone you're friendly with as a colleague. Remember it's difficult for the interviewer too, but they're not assessing you on your niceness, only in relation to the job. Be friendly, but businesslike. Keep a formal tone, and present your evidence just as you would at an ordinary interview. It may help to dress up for the occasion to show that you appreciate the ground rules.

Interviews for postgraduate study

If you're applying for a *vocational* course, e.g. interpreting and translating, these interviews may be very similar to job interviews, and will look at your wider experiences and career plans. (If you're going for a seemingly vocational course it's also worth asking what graduates from the course go on to do: does it deliver in terms of enhanced career prospects? Do they assume it does, or do they have evidence – such as a past graduate you can talk to?)

If you're applying for an *academic* course, or a research degree, then the interviewer will concentrate on your studies – the depth and breadth of your undergraduate degree. Prepare to discuss your dissertation or projected research field in some detail. You may also be asked how you hope to fund your studies, so your preparatory research should cover sources of funding. You may also want to ask the interviewer how people are normally funded on this course, and if the institution has any bursaries of its own.

Sometimes graduates have a starry-eyed view of postgraduate study: remember that universities, too, operate in a market and need to fill their courses. It's worth researching whether a course would actually deliver what you hope for.

Your university careers service will have many books, files and videos on attending interviews. See the Further information section at the end of this book.

Summary

• Being well prepared will give you confidence.
• Work out the evidence you're going to present and determine to get your strongest points across.
• Show you understand the business context the employer operates in.
• Practice open and confident body language.
• Show enthusiasm for the job.

Second interviews / selection centres

Some employers have more than one interview stage and will use first interviews as a preselection for their final intensive selection. (This includes almost all major employers participating in the Milk Round campus visits.) This second interview stage will usually last one or two days, and will often be based at the employer's premises; sometimes (for larger employers) it's at a special selection or training centre. This second stage, or selection board, will most likely involve candidates in a variety of tasks, sometimes working together.

If you get invited to an intensive selection board you may well be given a timetable and possibly an indication of what to expect. You may, for example, be asked to prepare a presentation or to read a set of documents in advance. It is very important that you follow the instructions carefully and prepare as thoroughly as possible.

Here are some examples of events, tasks and exercises you may encounter at second interview. (You are unlikely to encounter all of them!)

Group exercises

These require you to work with other candidates on a variety of *tasks*. This is to see how well you work with other people: what role you adopt in the group; whether you are cooperative; creative; assertive about putting your ideas forward; able to listen to others' ideas; etc. You may be given different roles in different exercises – taking it in turns to be leader, chairperson or whatever. The important thing to remember is to work *with* the other candidates, not against them. Bear in mind that good managers have to bring out the best in other people, not ride roughshod over them. You might not even be competing against the other candidates – some organizations – especially if they have several vacancies – recruit to a standard rather than looking for a 'top dog' – and might take *all* your group, or none!

Always take the tasks seriously – even if they involve balloons, straws or Lego men. Here are examples of exercises:

- Groups of candidates were asked to make an exact copy of a Lego man. The sample was in a separate room, and only one member of a group at a time was allowed to see it – and then only for a very short period. This person then had to give information back to the group. The winning team was the one that built a Lego model most like the original, within the time allocated.
- Candidates had to move coloured ping-pong balls from one set of bins into another as quickly as possible by colour coding them and obeying increasingly restrictive and complex instructions. Only the leader was given the instructions, and they had to memorize them. Leaders changed with each turn, when the 'rules' also changed.

Obviously, the point of these exercises was not to create a Lego man or to sort ping-pong balls, but to see how the candidates communicated and worked as a team: defining the problem; putting forward solutions; negotiating tasks; adapting strategies when necessary; and working with a sense of urgency.

You might be given a *role* to play in a realistic work situation (e.g. each candidate is a department head who has to make their case for a share of a limited budget). Keep in mind what you are trying to achieve and the time limits. If chairing the meeting, make sure everyone is heard; if someone is dominating summarize their position and move on; keep returning to the main objective; keep your eye on the clock and set a time at which a decision must be made. (You could prepare by looking at information on conducting and chairing meetings; look in the business section of the library).

Always listen carefully to the precise objective of each exercise, especially in group tasks. For example, if you have to build the tallest tower, it may not need to be the most stable – just the tallest.

Usually, in group exercises, assessors will be allocated to each candidate, noting their behaviour and input.

Written exercises or problem-solving exercises

These usually also test your communication and time management skills. For example, you may be given a hypothetical case related to the work you are applying for: trainee journalists might have a story to write within a given time; personnel applicants may be given papers outlining a problem (e.g. an employee's persistent 'sickness') and have to suggest different approaches. Here's an example from sales:

- *Sam is one of your best salespeople. He sells almost twice as much as anyone else, but this is causing resentment within the sales team, particularly as it is alleged he takes Fridays off. You are his manager: what do you do?*

You are being required to analyse and evaluate the information, and come up with possible solutions, all the time exercising your judgment.

Several things may be being tested in these exercises: sense of urgency; ability to absorb information quickly; ability to prioritize; ability to write clearly; ability to make decisions . . .

In-tray exercises

These involve working with several problems at once, often presented in different ways, e.g. by email, telephone, letter, memo, etc. Again this involves problem-solving and exercising judgement. Importantly, they require you to prioritize tasks, showing you can appreciate different levels of importance and urgency (urgent isn't always important and vice versa). Selectors are looking at the ability to grasp essential information quickly, take decisions under pressure and show a sense of urgency.

Drafting exercises

These are a way of testing your written communication skills. Can you express information clearly and tactfully? An example task might be:

A benefactor has given the local hospital a valuable painting to be displayed in the reception foyer. However, the subject matter is gory and totally unsuitable for a hospital. You have to write a letter tactfully declining the gift.

Presentations

You might be asked to prepare a presentation in advance or be given a limited time to prepare during the selection process – in this case your time management is being assessed as much as your ability to give a good presentation. Most students these days have experience of presentations in their course work, but here's a reminder of some useful questions to ask yourself:

- Who is the talk for? (*The group? Specialists?*)
- What is it for? (*To inform? To entertain?*)

The content, structure and style of the presentation will depend on its purpose and context. For example, if you're asked to give a general talk on any topic of your choice, then choose something of potential interest to the audience, and use non-technical language. Some points to think about are:

1 Structure it carefully and let the audience know what to expect.

- introduce yourself;
- introduce the topic;
- give an overview of the structure.

2 Keep to the point and talk off-the-cuff or from brief notes. One good tip is to use visual aids (e.g. PowerPoint or flip chart notes) as a reminder of what to talk about, and in what order. The audience will like them and won't realize that they're there for your benefit not theirs. Never read from a script – this is very boring and you won't

have any rapport at all with your audience, because you won't be able to look at them.

3 Smile, look at and respond to the audience.

4 Liven things up with visual aids (e.g. by passing something round, using PowerPoint or giving visual examples from web sources).

5 Stick rigidly to the time limit given. Don't make it too short or too long – however entertaining you think it is!

6 Have a clear conclusion (e.g. *'In conclusion, solar power must be the energy of the future . . .'*) and then summarize the key points.

Tests or questionnaires

Some employers use tests or questionnaires as a supplement to other selection procedures. These could be straightforward *physical tests*, e.g. of colour blindness or spacial awareness (RAF fliers, for example, are tested for their fast reactions and physical coordination). Or they could try to gain an insight into your *personality* or to assess your *performance* in particular tasks – for example, tests of logical reasoning.

There are two main types of written test:

1 Those that try to elicit *information about your personality*, such as your aptitudes, beliefs or what motivates you (e.g. *Is this person outgoing, decisive, a risk taker?* – or whatever the job requires). These are usually not timed and there are no specifically 'right' or 'wrong' answers; they will be looking for people who seem to fit the personal profile appropriate for the job.

   You can't usually prepare for these tests, and the best advice is to answer honestly – although you may suspect that some answers might be more helpful than others!

2 Those that *test your performance* in a particular type of task (e.g. verbal, numerical or logical reasoning, data sufficiency). These are often against the clock and you may be given more questions than you can finish. Do read the instructions carefully.

   You may be given access to practice sheets before the tests to enable you to familiarize yourself with them: take this opportunity to be absolutely clear about what you need to do. Timing should not start until all the instructions are given and the examples worked through.

You should ideally be told what types of test you will be given, what they are used for and who will see the results. The British Psychological Society also recommends that you be given feedback on the results.

Examples of tests and questionnaires can be found on many websites, including those of Prospects and the British Psychological Society (see Further information at the end of this book). You are unlikely to be required to do high level maths, unless it's part of the job requirement, but basic numeracy is often required. If you're rusty, it may help to look at 'refresher' books or just to practice basic arithmetic.

If you have any kind of disability which requires special conditions, tell the organization as soon as you know about the test session.

Discussions

These will usually be based on a problem related to the type of job you're going for. For example:

> *Fred has put in false expense claims. He has been staying with his sister but claimed hotel bills. When asked about it, he was quite open about what he had done, and said he thought it was okay as he only claimed the lowest rate, and paid the money to his sister. What should you, his manager, do?*

Sometimes there are no easy solutions to these problems; the point is to assess the quality of your ideas, how you listen to and use others' ideas and the maturity of the judgements you make.

One to one interviews

Occasionally you may have more one-to-one interviews; these could be with people you would be working for, specialists or psychologists. Treat them as you would any interview (see 'Interviews' earlier in this chapter, p. 111), prepare as well as you can and try to avoid getting flustered. The interviewer might deliberately try to apply pressure to see how you react (if the job is very stressful, for example); remain polite, friendly and calm whatever the circumstances.

Talks and tours

The employer may give a presentation about the company or a visit around the site. Stay focused during these. Just occasionally they will test you on what you've learned. You can also be finding things out for yourself in order to decide whether you would want to work here.

Assume you're being assessed all the time by everyone you meet.

If a factory or site tour is part of the timetable, you may need to take safe and comfortable shoes.

Social events

Work usually requires us to adopt a series of roles or personae: you wouldn't behave at work, for example, as you would in a club with your friends. The idea of 'decorum', or appropriate behaviour, may not be hugely fashionable these days, but it does still apply. In your working life you will probably find yourself in situations where you are seen as the representative of your employer. Embedding social events into selection is a way of finding out how you comport yourself. It may be a useful job skill, for example, to mix easily with new acquaintances.

Candidates might be given 40 minutes in the bar before dinner to 'mix and mingle' with recent graduate employees; this gives you the chance to find out more about the job and the company, and gives the employer the chance to see what you are like in a social situation. Formal meals aren't there to see if you know which fork to use, but how you carry yourself and how well you mix with others. It's always a good idea to go easy on the alcohol – it has been known for employers to provide a free bar to candidates in the evening, and then at the last minute to ask them to prepare a talk for first thing the following morning!

There may not be any formal assessment going on at social events, but selectors will be gaining impressions of the candidates.

Selection centres can be hugely challenging, but fun. Many students say they were reassured by the rigour of the selection – it gave them confidence that, if appointed, they would actually be up to the job! Try to enjoy yourself and learn as much as you can.

Summary

- If you're sent papers before the selection day, read them carefully and prepare any exercises.
- Assume that you're being assessed from the moment you walk through the gate until the moment you leave – whoever you meet.
- Always listen carefully to the precise objective of each exercise, especially in group tasks.
- Remember, your time management skills are being assessed, including your sense of urgency. Work is less freewheeling than student life!

6

Lifetime career skills

After Graduation: Leaving University moving on; Getting a job offer; Making decisions; Negotiating; Troubleshooting – where am I going wrong? • Creating The Life You Want: Achieving your ambitions; Recognizing opportunities; Building your confidence

This section is divided into two parts: the first looks at some of the skills, strategies and information you might need soon after graduation; the second aims to give you tips about managing your career throughout your working life.

After graduation

Leaving university, moving on

> *Where the old tracks are lost, new country is revealed with all its wonders . . .*
>
> (Rabindranath Tagore)

Most people know that the loss of regular work can be as traumatic as bereavement (in fact people often go through similar stages – of anger, denial, despair, acceptance – as in bereavement) and the departure from student life can be equally difficult, involving loss of routine, status, defined goals and being apart from your friends. Here are some coping strategies:

1 *Accept the new situation.* Use graduation as a rite of passage from student to worker (or invent your own rite). Keep some symbols of your past, get rid of others. Remind yourself also of the continuities in your life, such as:

   • the friends you are still in touch with
   • subject expertise that you can continue independently
   • hobbies/ interests you can still pursue

   Accept also, that it's time to move on to new challenges.

2 *Know your own needs.* In Chapter 3 you identified your key values. You need to take steps to meet these, if possible. For example, if your need is to contribute to something valuable or to make friends, you could try voluntary work to meet these needs while you are job-hunting. Try to formulate a plan by which you can meet these needs in some area of your life. If you are a person who finds life difficult without a routine, for example, make your own timetable involving job-hunting, chores, leisure activities, etc.

3 *Formulate an action plan.* It's important not to lapse into apathy but to keep yourself motivated, and to keep active in your job-hunting. Identify step by step actions you could take to move yourself forward, for example,

   • in satisfying your key values (*e.g. getting voluntary or temporary work*);
   • in improving your job-chances (*e.g. I need to get experience working with children*).

   (See more about action planning later, in 'Creating the life you want', p. 147.)

4 *Boost your confidence.* Most people lose confidence very quickly, especially when faced with unemployment. Maintain yours by understanding that your position will not be unique and is not necessarily the result of your own inadequacies. Most new graduates take some time to find a 'proper' job, especially if they are applying for very competitive fields. (Similarly, during your career you might be made redundant because of a recession, a take-over or other factors beyond

your control. At times like these, again, you will need to maintain confidence.)

See later, in 'Creating the life you want' (p. 149), for tips on building confidence. One useful strategy is to try to join a support group – this could be your family, friends or a job-hunting circle. Use this group to give and receive feedback and encouragement. (But don't join together to moan – this will only demoralize you.)

5 *Recognize opportunities.* Seize any chances – to learn, to make contacts, to develop new skills . . . (See later in this chapter, pp. 148–9.)

> Josie graduated with an excellent arts degree but because of personal circumstances was living in a rural area with little employment. Then someone remarked that she seemed to know a lot about plants . . . would she do their garden? (Her grandfather was a gardener and she had learned a lot without realizing it.) She did a few hours a week, but soon had more work than she could cope with. She began to get more ambitious – planning a new garden, building ponds and finally did a professional landscaping course. She now runs her own garden design business.

Getting a job offer

It's wonderful when, after all the effort of job searching, making applications and going to interviews, you get a letter offering you a job.

It can also be stressful because you will be making a big decision. Suddenly the hypothetical situation, imagining yourself in the job, is about to become real. This might be exhilarating or it might be scary (often both). You might even have other applications in the pipeline and be undecided whether to accept this one. So what do you do?

Accepting a job offer

Even if you have been made an offer orally, the employer should follow this up with a letter formally offering you the job. This letter will probably include:

- name of the employing organization
- date of the offer
- job title/department/location
- salary
- hours of work

- starting date (this might be negotiable)
- location you will be working at
- period of notice required for either party to terminate the contract

and it may include:

- details of other conditions of service, such as holidays, pension information, 'perks' and possibly any important rules you are asked to undertake to keep (e.g. confidentiality).

It should be signed by someone authorized to make the offer, such as a Human Resources manager.

Sometimes you may get an offer which is *conditional* upon, say: getting a minimum class of degree; a medical examination; a probationary period; or that you accept the job by a particular date.

Keep this letter as it makes up half of your contract of employment.

The second half is your letter of acceptance. Write as soon as you can to the person who sent the offer letter (giving their reference number or code if there is one). Say you accept the post of [give the job title] under the terms outlined in their letter of [date] and agree to start on [give starting date agreed by both parties].

As the word contract indicates, if you accept a job you are making a legal undertaking. You should not accept a job with the intention of rejecting it later if something better turns up (see the code of practice agreed between the Association of Graduate Careers Advisory Services, the National Union of Students and the Association of Graduate Recruiters on www. agcas.csu.ac.uk).

Rejecting a job offer

Reply immediately referring to their letter (date and reference as above) politely declining the offer. You might want to give a reason, but you don't have to. Write *immediately* as this gives them the chance to offer the job to someone else; and *politely* because, even if you had a bad experience, you never know if you'll want to work for them in the future!

What if you can't decide?

Here are some typical problems:

1 *You're not clear* about something or *you can't meet their exact*

requirements (e.g. you might have booked a holiday which means you can't make the starting date).

Telephone the person sending you the letter without delay to ask for more information or to try to negotiate around the problem.

2 *Is it really what you want?* Like getting married, job offers tend to cause at least a few moments of having cold feet! Starting something new is always challenging and a little risky (think about when you started university). If you have done your research on what you personally would like in a job and what this job offers, you will at least have the information to weigh up the pros and cons. You have put all this effort into getting the job, *they* think you can do it, so do think carefully before declining without giving it a try.

3 *You've just seen the holiday entitlement!* Holidays are always a shock after years as a student. It can seem as if work is a prison sentence. Don't forget that there are such things as Bank holidays and weekends – and that many people actually enjoy their work!

4 *You have other applications in the pipeline.* Your options are to make a decision or to try to stall. If you choose the latter, ring the employer who is making the offer, explain the situation and ask how soon they need a decision. You might, however, ask yourself:

- How far along in the pipeline is the other job? Do you just have a vague hope of an interview or is there a possible job offer? Could you ring the second employer and ask if they could give any indication of whether you are on the short list for an offer (or interview)?

  If you were offered both jobs ask yourself which would you take? If it is this one, accept it now. (This sounds obvious, but some people do hang on waiting for offers because they like to feel wanted.)

- Do you need more information about either job? Try to get it immediately.

- Remember – 'a bird in the hand is worth two in the bush' – what would you feel if you rejected this and *didn't* get the other? (See the decision making box below.)

- It may help to discuss the situation with someone impartial like a careers adviser. But do it quickly.

5 *You're scared of committing yourself.* No job is a life sentence. If, after giving it a good try, you really don't like the job, you can resign. (Or, in a large organization, you can see if you can be moved to a different job. At this stage they'll have invested in your training so may be keen to keep you.) You will certainly have learned something by doing the

job even if you decide it's not for you, and the experience might be useful in getting other jobs. However, if you change jobs frequently, employers will recognize this as a pattern and it will become difficult to get long-term employment.

Thinking points

- No job will ever be perfect, there will always be parts we like and others we dislike.
- Sometimes it's the parts of the job we're slightly scared about that really stretch us and become most personally rewarding because they force us to 'grow'.
- Few organizations expect you to hit the ground running; most will offer some sort of training or period of support. If they do expect you to be a fast starter, they will have made this clear in the assessment process.
- Your indecision might result from anxiety or lack of confidence rather than any real preference. Remember – if they've offered you the job they have good reasons to think *you can do it.*
- Do a risk/benefit analysis. Itemize what you are risking and what you stand to gain. It's human nature to exaggerate the risks (see below).

Making decisions

Some people make decisions easily and confidently. Others are paralysed by 'What if . . .' and either don't make the decision at all or procrastinate for so long that the opportunity has gone. If, as predicted (see Chapter 2), people can expect to change jobs more frequently throughout their working lives, decision–making, (including the ability to see and seize opportunities), will become an important 'career skill'. Susan Jeffers in her book *Feel the Fear and Do It Anyway* posits a very useful model for decision making. She says we often see decisions as being polarized as either 'right' or 'wrong':

DECISION →   wrong   ☹
       →   right   ☺

but in fact few decisions in life are like this. Often if we make a 'wrong' decision, it leads to new and better places. She suggests a better paradigm:

DECISION →   opportunity   ☺
          →   opportunity   ☺

In other words, all opportunities lead to other opportunities if you can make the best of them.

Simone was a graduate in her mid-30s. She enjoyed her job but was in a bit of a rut, so when her partner was offered promotion in a different area of the country she willingly moved, and started a completely different kind of job. She hated it and found it mentally and emotionally draining. However she stuck at it for two years before applying for, and getting, a job she came to really love. *She got this second job principally because of the experience she had gained doing the job she hated.*

It's almost invariably fruitless to dwell on what might have been. By all means reflect on decisions and learn from mistakes, but always move on and make the best of where you are. Here are some helps and hindrances when making decisions:

Helps

- Be aware of your own feelings and values
- Investigate your options
- Know your priorities
- Make a provisional decision; sometimes this clarifies your feelings
- Make the decision and commit to it; stay optimistic about your choice

Hindrances

- Thinking there is always only one correct choice
- Not having enough information
- Feeling depressed or having low self-esteem
- Wanting everything
- Panic
- Dwelling on what might have been.

Sometimes students who have been unemployed for a while find it hard to accept a job offer, simply because their confidence is low and they feel they can't do the job. If you've been offered it, *you probably can*. What have you got to lose? What have you got to gain?

> *In my experience, one factor blocking students' ability to make any career decision at all is a fear that making the 'wrong' choice will slam all other doors shut. In my view, going into one career option often opens up other doors, rather than closing them.*
>
> (University careers adviser)

Different people find different things risky: one might happily back-pack round the world but quake at getting married; another might love hang-gliding but would faint if asked to do a karaoke turn. Risks come in different forms: emotional (asking someone out); physical (surfing); social (wearing the 'wrong' clothes); financial (borrowing money); etc. It's always useful to do a mini-cost/benefit analysis: ask yourself:

- *What could I lose?* And
- *What might I gain?*

Often we mentally exaggerate what we have to lose. For example, some students are fearful of asking for information interviews, but what's the worst thing that could happen (the person you ask says no)? And what's the best thing that could happen (*you would gain priceless information and make new contacts*)?

Here's one model to aid decision making:

1 Awareness:

- be aware of your overall objective: why you need to make the decision.
- remember that few decisions are 'right' or 'wrong'.

2 Information:

- gather information about each choice as far as time will allow;
- work out possible options, risks and benefits.

3 Evaluation:

- assess the choices in relation to your goals, feelings, priorities.
- choose.
- if stuck make a provisional choice and test what it 'feels' like.

4 Action:

- put your choice into action;
- commit to it.

You can transform a potentially good decision into a bad one by not putting any effort behind it. Alternatively, you can make almost any decision a 'good' one by pursuing it wholeheartedly.

> *An option becomes a decision through the process of dedicating ourselves to it.*
>
> (T.I. Rubin 1990)

Negotiating

Today's gradates may face many changes in their working lives. They may also enter work not previously done by graduates, or may need to negotiate with their boss over pay, promotion or to enlarge or develop the job they are doing. The ability to negotiate successfully can be a key career skill. Here are a few short notes to help you develop your negotiation skills.

Negotiating is often seen as involving two opposing factions pushing against each other – like two stags fighting – until one gives way. It need not always be like this. In fact it's sometimes more fruitful to approach negotiations as presenting a situation requiring *joint problem-solving*. This way you focus on the issue under discussion and are better able to maintain the relationship between you and the other party, which is as, or more, important than getting your preferred outcome.

Approaching a negotiation

1 Try to arrange the meeting when the other party won't be in a bad mood or in a hurry (unless you think that in this situation they'll say 'yes' just to get rid of you!)
2 Make sure you can clearly express what you want and why. For example, if you want to be sent on a training course, can you explain what it involves and what it will enable you to do or contribute? (You might not want to disclose your whole agenda at once – if you were buying a used car from someone you wouldn't usually offer your top price straight away.)
3 Ask yourself – is what I want realistic? Is it something the other party can give? E.g.

Employer:	*Where is this training course?*
You:	*Majorca.*
Employer:	*Isn't there one in Croydon?*

4 Think about what the other party might want and whether or not it conflicts with what you want. What might be influencing them – pressure from someone else? The need to save face and be seen to have negotiated strongly? E.g.

Employer: *You are a good worker, with potential. I would like to send you on this course but won't all the others on your section want to go if you go?*

You: *I gave presentations at college and think I'm good at communicating. If I do this course I can offer training sessions to the others when I get back, to make it worth your while sending me.*

Listen carefully to what the other party is saying and try to pick up any other signals, i.e., non-verbal signals which might give you a clue to their position.

5 Brainstorm ideas and think of as many options as you can. What other ways might you meet your objective? E.g.

- *I could go to night school.*
- *We could ask for a trainer to come for one day to work with us all.*
- *I could be seconded to another department for a while.*
- *Does anyone else on this section want to learn this?*

When you have gathered as many ideas as you can, evaluate the most promising – which would the other party find most convincing? These could be your back-up arguments.

6 Use objective facts, if possible, or establish the principle behind your position. E.g.

- *Andy and Mike took a similar course last year. Amanda and I were expecting to get our chance this year.*
- *The handbook says a Ford Fiesta of this year with a similar mileage is usually around £3,900 . . .*

7 Be positive. Don't go into a negotiation expecting to fail.

If the negotiation stalls it's best to appeal to principles or objective criteria rather than make it an ego issue. *(It's not fair!)* Accept that some things are unobtainable and have a realistic idea of other options if necessary.

Tips

- Focus on problem-solving and keep things objective.
- Think of possible objections to what you want and how you might overcome them.
- Be positive.

Troubleshooting – where am I going wrong?

Here are some common problems, with strategies for finding solutions.

There aren't any vacancies

The problem might be that you are not looking in the right places.

Do you know where these jobs are advertised? Look again at Chapter 4 and start researching and information interviewing. Remember that not all jobs are advertised.

Some very popular jobs are never advertised at all, because so many people make speculative applications that there's no need for employers to advertise them. Consider the creative job-hunting route (see Chapter 4); but do consider that these jobs may well be extremely competitive. It may be the sort of job where you would be advised to try to 'get a foot in the door' – in whatever capacity.

I'm not getting interviews

Many new graduates underestimate how difficult it is to get that first job, and therefore don't put nearly enough effort into *crafting the best possible application form or CV*. Examine Chapter 5, 'Application forms' and 'Interviews' in detail (see pp. 78–111). Have you really done the groundwork, investigating the jobs you're applying for? Is the evidence you present clear and convincing? If possible, ask someone to give you feedback on your application forms and CV (your careers service may be able to help).

Alternatively it could be that your application form and CV are good, but you haven't sufficient hard evidence to convince an employer you're worth interviewing. In this case you could:

- gain more experience, e.g. through voluntary work;
- boost your skills or qualifications, e.g. though short courses; or
- it might be worth trying to enter the field at a lesser level.

Another possible reason for not getting interviews is that you're applying for very competitive jobs. Some jobs are more popular than others. Seemingly glamorous jobs in TV, film or the music industry, for example, attract thousands of applicants and are very difficult to get into. Even in more mainstream jobs there are fads and fashions in applications: human resources management, for example, currently tends to attract more applicants than production management.

It may be worth looking at Chapter 4 again with a view to widening your options. Are there other job areas that you're not considering? Or you might consider the creative job-hunting strategy or looking to enter in any capacity (as suggested earlier).

You might be applying for too senior a position. It may be worth enquiring before applying if the position would be suitable for a new graduate. If not, they might be able to suggest more appropriate entry-level grades. Bear in mind what was discussed in Chapter 2: being a graduate isn't necessarily an instant passport into a great job; you may have to work your way up to it.

You might be wrong for the jobs you are applying for. It's often difficult to estimate our own abilities or experiences in relation to the requirements of a job. This is particularly true if it's your first 'proper' job. (And sometimes employers reject people who they consider are too qualified or even too able, on the grounds that they're unlikely to stay.) It might be worth discussing what you're applying for with a careers adviser. Or you could try getting feedback on your chances of success from people doing the job, via information interviews (see Chapter 4). It may be worth going through Chapters 3 and 4 again, looking for alternative options.

I'm getting interviews but not job offers

Well, you're doing something right!

You might ask for *feedback* after a rejection, politely asking if there was any particular reason why you weren't chosen (e.g. *not enough experience of x?*) or if there's anything you might do to improve your interview technique? With this concrete information you may well be able to fix the problem. (Never rant – it will just confirm that they were right not to hire you.)

You might try to arrange a *mock interview* (some careers services are able to offer these, particularly in less busy times). Or practice interviewing and being interviewed with one, or preferably two, good friends. (One interviews, one is interviewed, one observes and gives clear and concise feedback.)

If you are repeatedly rejected, it may be that you are so good at 'selling yourself' on paper it's *disguising* the fact that you haven't enough experience, are applying for too senior a post, etc.

It may be that you *doubt your ability* to do the job and are unconsciously sabotaging your own efforts (it does happen). See 'Building your confidence' later in this chapter (pp. 149–151). If you really want the job, your enthusiasm will come across at interview.

I'm unemployed and getting desperate

Sometimes, however desperate you feel, you just need to persevere (perseverance is one of the key elements of success in any sphere of activity). However, it is often helpful to be open to different ideas, to look for different types of work, or for alternative ways into the job you want. You may need to work through Chapters 3 and 4 again, trying to widen your options and get new ideas about jobs you might be suited to and job-hunting strategies. Do use feedback from others, such as careers advisers, to find out if your applications are good enough.

Above all, you need to maintain your confidence: a good way would be to get involved in voluntary work – there are many organizations (such as Community Service Volunteers) offering different types of work. You can make contacts, use your talents in a good cause, learn new skills, and avoid that awkward 'unemployed' gap in your CV.

Creating the life you want

Your attitudes are important in achieving your ambitions. People who are happy with their lives and achievements often share key approaches to living. They tend to be:

- people who set themselves clear achievable goals
- people who persevere in the face of difficulties, who don't easily get discouraged
- people who see achievement as being a result of effort rather than the inevitable flowering of some innate ability
- people who value all experiences as a chance to learn, and don't label their actions as 'successes' or 'failures'

Here are a few tips on how you can cultivate these positive approaches.

Achieving your ambitions

> *Where there is no vision, people perish.*
>
> (Proverbs 29:18)

Some people just know how to set goals and achieve them. Others have vague wishes – things they would like, but never do much about. Sometimes people don't succeed in their ambitions for one of these reasons:

- they're unclear about what they actually want
- they don't know how to achieve it
- they're not motivated enough to do anything about it

Equally, many people have dreams which they dismiss as fantasies because they assume they're impossible – *without ever testing whether this is in fact true.*

> *I always wanted to be a writer. I didn't think it was possible. Then I did an information interview with a 'real' writer – a novelist. I was shocked how little money she made – she had other jobs. But she did say to me that if you want to be a writer, write – it's as simple as that.*
>
> (Benjamin)

Having your own personal goals or objectives can give you direction, energy and purpose. They can help you test out your dreams because they deal with practicalities and test your commitment. Make sure your objectives *are* your own – it's easy to be influenced by others, consciously or not.

> Lesley was a mature student who was finding it hard to get accepted on a teaching course. In discussion it emerged that she had always been in the shadow of her elder brother who was now a headmaster and the family 'success story' – she felt she didn't matter. She consciously re-evaluated her intention of becoming a teacher – was it really her own personal goal or was she trying to compete with her brother? After much thought and several information interviews she decided she did really want to teach, but her personal aim was to teach hearing-impaired

> children. It was this she wanted, even more than status within the family. With her goals clear she was much more highly motivated to make successful applications.

Objectives can be short- or long-term (e.g. *to arrange an information interview by next week; to have children before I'm 40; to write a collection of songs; to spend an hour every evening playing with the kids*) and can be in any area of your life. Having objectives doesn't mean you should be driven or workaholic – in fact, clear objectives can help you manage your time more effectively so you enjoy the things that are important to you.

Here are five tips on setting personal objectives:

1 *Be as precise as possible* so you know what you are going for and can tell when you have achieved it. For example, *'To work hard at my dissertation'* is vague whereas *'to finish Chapter 3 by 1st May'* is specific. *'To take a year out'* is vague *'to spend up to a year travelling, supporting myself by working as I go'* is getting a firmer grasp of what you need to do.
2 *Be realistic.* Think about how long it will really take, or whether you have the capacity to achieve your objective. Don't set yourself up to fail. Sometimes students focus on superficially 'glamorous' career options without investigating what they really demand. Or they set impossible targets: *'to finish the essay by tomorrow'*, when they haven't even started the reading! The more informed you are, the more focused your goals will be.
3 *Give it a time limit.* Otherwise it will be one of those things you mean to do, someday. *'Write a short story every week'* (this was Ray Bradbury's method when starting out); *'send my CV to three potential employers by Friday'*. If you're hoping to get into a very competitive field, it might be useful to set yourself a time limit after which you will examine other options, or alternative ways in.
4 *Motivate yourself.* Think of the advantages that achieving your objective will bring, and imagine how you will feel. (If you feel apprehensive it may be worth rethinking whether this goal really is appropriate for you). Give yourself rewards when you achieve your objectives.

> Verne slogged through his PhD by sticking a picture on the wall above his desk – it was the canoe he promised himself when he got his Doctorate.

> Julie's dissertation hung over her for months. She wrote it by having a treat – a nice meal or day out – every time she finished a chapter, and by focusing on the feeling of relief and achievement at being one step closer to finishing.

5 If necessary, *do a cost/benefit analysis*. Write out what factors are working against you achieving your objective (and start brainstorming how to overcome them). Then write out what you have going for you, (and how you might boost these positives).

Action plans

> *Begin great things while they are easy.*
> *Do great things while they are small.*
> *The difficult things of the world must once have been easy.*
> *The great things must once have been small.*
> *A thousand mile journey begins with one step.*
>
>   (Lao Tse)

Big, over-arching objectives can seem too daunting to be possible, so break them down into achievable action plans. Action plans are built from small steps. For example, I might dream of being prime minister, which may seem impossible – but my immediate action could be to join a political party, which is easy.

If your objective is to take a year out working and travelling, then your immediate action plan may involve:

* Applying for a passport
* Starting to plan an itinerary
* Investigating work options and visa requirements in different countries
* Researching cheap flights
* Reading up on working overseas in the careers library

Action plans should be precise, logical and practical. Always start with what you are going to do *now* and follow it up with a realistic timescale. Be creative, brainstorm as many strategies as possible – ask friends and family for suggestions. Often, we can't see possibilities but others can. If, for example, you are hoping to work in a very competitive field, there are often 'back doors' or alternative routes in, if you can be flexible and creative enough.

If you persistently set yourself small goals and achieve them, you will have built the habit of success. (Conversely, failure breeds failure.)

> *Sow a thought, reap an action.*
> *Sow an action, reap a habit.*
> *Sow a habit, reap a character.*
> *Sow a character, reap a destiny.*

Perseverance can be the difference between success and disappointment. However it is also necessary to be flexible and to re-evaluate your objectives – circumstances change and so might you!

Recognizing opportunities

Sometimes, people let opportunities pass them by simply because they don't recognize them as opportunities.

> *When I was young, I was invited to read my poetry at [a large] university. The organizer, one of the dons, asked the three of us [poets] to his rooms next morning for an informal breakfast. I was too shy to go. This man had contacts throughout the literary world. It took me years to realize what an opportunity I'd wasted.*
>
> (Paul, poet and playwright)

Learn

Any chance to learn something is an opportunity. If given the chance, go on courses, learn new things. You never know where they might lead, or when they might be useful.

> *The British have the wrong attitude to training. If the company picks someone for a training course, people often say 'Why? What's wrong with the way I do it now?' whereas workers in other countries would see being chosen as a benefit or distinction.*
>
> (Company training manager)

Get involved

A chance to get involved in something could be an opportunity.

Committees, societies and local community groups could give you valuable experience, help build your confidence and can be used for making contacts.

Find out

A chance to find out, information interview or 'network' is an opportunity.

> A speaker at a graduate employability conference told this story:
> He had invited six new graduates for a working lunch as a 'consolation prize' for not getting a job they had been short-listed for. Only one turned up. The speaker had intended to help them all with their career plans, and if possible, introduce them to other contacts. By not replying promptly or seeing this lunch (however daunting) as an opportunity, the graduates had lost valuable chances.

Other people

Other people can provide opportunities. Is there someone you know or someone in the organization you already work for, who can help you – giving tips, pointers or advice?

> *Mentor – a wise and trusted adviser or guide*
>
> (Dictionary definition)

Building your confidence

> *'Our doubts are traitors*
> *And make us lose the good we oft might win*
> *By fearing to attempt.'*
>
> (Shakespeare)

Confidence has been described as an essential attribute for success: if you have talents, but haven't got the confidence to use them, they're not much use to you. However, many people lack confidence, especially when making the transition from study to work. It sometimes seems that everyone else is supremely confident – whereas the truth is, for most of us, confidence is tidal – it comes in and it goes out!

Here are a few tips on building confidence:

Think positively

Most of us have an inner critical voice in our head, commenting on our inadequacies. Many women, in particular, say that they often feel 'a fraud' and are afraid of being 'found out' even when they're functioning perfectly well. This negative voice is demoralizing and useless: don't allow it to speak. Allow yourself a positive, encouraging voice, e.g. *'This interview is going well . . . I am calm and relaxed . . .'*

If you go into an interview thinking, *'I'm useless'*, your negative attitude will come over in your voice, body language and statements. But if mental attitude works in a negative way (and it does) it can also work in a positive way, so always think positive (*'I can do this'*). Another tip is to always make statements in the present tense ('I *am* successful'). Try it and see what happens.

Celebrate your strengths

When we do something well, we often assume it's something *everyone* can do. But, oddly, if we find something difficult, it's easy to think 'I'm the *only* person who finds this hard!' Of course both of these assumptions are quite wrong. Look at the skills lists you made in Chapter 3, recognize the things you do well and allow yourself to feel good about them. Do things you know you can do well. What projects or voluntary work might utilize these skills?

Have a go

We develop confidence by doing. Even if something doesn't work out – you tried! You don't have to be a genius and you don't have to be perfect. What matters is being willing and constructive. 'Have a go' and if you make mistakes, learn from them. When starting something daunting, think of it as fun. This can radically change your approach to it.

Set yourself goals

One great way of building confidence is to set yourself achievable goals (as discussed earlier). Achievements, however small, act as stepping stones to confidence; success really does build success. Conversely, if you fall into a habit of setting yourself half-hearted goals and not achieving them this will demoralize you. Make yourself try new things and meet new people. Devise your own challenges, and succeed at them.

Look and act the part

How you regard yourself affects the way other people treat you, so pay attention to dress, grooming and how you present yourself to the world. Have a positive mental image of who you want to be and act as if you were that person. Don't be afraid to adopt the appropriate role for different situations – we all have to use different roles in different aspects of our lives.

University life can be challenging – even daunting. Remember how you felt on day one? But overcoming challenges is how we build confidence. Most students feel that during their studies they have learned a lot, widened their mental outlook, built confidence through a track record of success and 'grown' both professionally and personally.

7

Final word

Getting work you enjoy after graduation can sometimes be a long and challenging process: students often under-estimate just how much effort is required. However, you should now have the career skills to look for alternative jobs at any stage of your life.

Here are a few tips:

- Keep your CV up to date. You will otherwise forget things you've done, training you've had, even qualifications you've obtained. Make sure you keep recording your achievements as your career develops.
- You are responsible for your own career path. There are many things which we can't control, but there are many that we can. If you find yourself in a rut or hating your job, do something about it. Go through some of the Chapter 3 exercises again – is it every aspect of the job you hate, or just some? What might you do to change it?
- Use all the resources available to you – friends, family, your careers service – for ideas, information, contacts, feedback and support.

Many undergraduates go to their careers service naively expecting to be told 'what to be'. My answer always (unhelpfully) was 'be happy'. Getting work you enjoy is important in building your happiness, but other things are important too. Keep your personal values in mind and the things you really enjoy, and try to build them in to your life.

> *What you can do, or dream you can, begin it;*
> *Boldness has genius, power and magic in it.*
>
> (Goethe)

Further information

A comprehensive website covering career choice, job-hunting, vacancies, self-employment, voluntary work, time out, postgraduate study, etc. is www.prospects.ac.uk – supported by university careers services.

Your University Careers Service will be an invaluable resource for all types of opportunities. There are many information leaflets and brochures available on occupations, vacancies, postgraduate study, taking a year out, vacation work, voluntary work, work placements, self-employment and working abroad. They will also hold books and videos on application forms, interviews and second interviews.

Other information sources are:

General

Bolles, R.N. (2006) *What Color Is Your Parachute*. Berkeley, CA: 10 Speed Press. (Pioneering and authoritative work on career choice and creative job-hunting.)
Hawkins, P. (1999) *The Art of Building Windmills*. Liverpool: GIEU, University of Liverpool.
Lees, J. (2005) *How to get a Job You'll Love*. Maidenhead: McGraw-Hill.
www.heacademy.ac.uk – comprehensive information on graduate employability

Help for particular groups of graduates

- National Bureau for students with disabilities: www.skill.org.uk
- Disability Rights Commission: www.drc.org.uk
- Employability for Black and Asian students: www.nrec.org.uk/employability and www.blackandasiangrad.ac.uk
- Employers Forum on Age: www.EFA.org.uk

What kind of work might you enjoy?

Eikleberry, C. (1995) *The Career Guide for Creative and Unconventional People.* Berkeley, CA: 10 Speed Press.

Francis, D. (1994) *Managing Your Own Career*: London: HarperCollins

Holland, J. *The Self Directed Search* available at www.self-directed-search.com

Hopson, B. and Scally, M. (2000*) Build Your Own Rainbow: A Workbook for Career and Life Management.* London: Management Books.

Myers, I. and Myers, P. (1993) *Gifts Differing: Understanding Personality Type.* Mountain View, CA: CPP Books.

Researching opportunities

Henderson G. and Henderson S. (eds) (1986) *The Directory of British Associations and Associations in Ireland.* Beckenham: CBD Research. (In most university libraries.)

Postgraduate study

- www.scholarship-search.org.uk
- www.npc.org.uk

Self employment

- www.businesslink.org
- www.artscouncil.org.uk
- www.scottisharts.org.uk
- www.artscouncil.wales.org.uk
- www.shell-livewire.org.uk
- www.smallbusiness.co.uk
- www.british-franchise.org.uk
- www.princes-trust.org.uk

Taking a year off

Flynn, M. (2002) *Taking a Year Off.* Richmond: Trotman.

Griffith, S. (2005) *Work Your Way Around the World.* Oxford: Vac Work Publications.

Vacancies

- www.prospects.co.uk
- www. doctorjob.com
- jobcentreplus.gov.uk.

For Local government vacancies:

- www.lgjobs.com
- www.agcasscotland.org.uk/graduates/local_authority.html

Presenting yourself effectively

AGCAS website: www.agcas.org.uk
Cole and Whistance (2004) *Creative CV Guide*. Guildford: Surrey Institute of Art & Design.
Hughes, M., McLoughlin and Nicholles (2001) *How To Write A Curriculum Vitae*. London: University of London Careers Service.
Pease, A. (1999) *Body Language*. London: Butterworth- Heinemann.
Pease, A. and Pease, B. (2004) *The Definitive Book of Body Language*. London: Orion.
Yeung, R. (2004) *Successful Interviews Every Time*. London: How To Books.

Tests and questionnaires

Try these websites for practice tests:

- www. prospects.ac.uk
- www.psychtesting.org.uk (British Psychological Society)
- www.totaljobs.com
- www.queendom.com
- www.work.guardian.co.uk/psychometrics

There are several 'refresher' books for numeracy tests, some of which your careers service may hold.

PGCE interviews

- www. dfes.gov.uk.
- www.teachernet.gov.uk
- www.nc.uk.net (National Curriculum)
- www.bbc.co.uk/schools

On organizational cultures

Handy, C. (2005) *Understanding Organisations*. London: Penguin
http://jobsearch.graduate.monster.co.uk

Lifetime career skills

For support networks look at the graduate forums on both the prospects and doctorjob websites.

Jeffers, S. (2002) *Feel the Fear and Do It Anyway*. London: Random House.
Rubin, T. (1993) *Overcoming Indecisiveness*. London: Hutchinson

Recommended by graduates

Finally, these were recommended to me by recent graduates:

Covey, S. (1999) *The 7 Habits of Highly Effective People*. New York: Simon & Shuster.
Harrold, F. (2001) *Be Your Own Life Coach*. London: Coronet.

Index